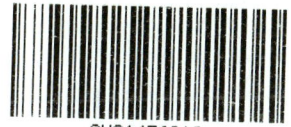

CW01456219

Protecting Our Planet Securing Our Future

Linkages Among Global Environmental Issues and Human Needs

Robert T. Watson

John A. Dixon

Steven P. Hamburg

Anthony C. Janetos

Richard H. Moss

November 1998

United Nations Environment Programme

U.S. National Aeronautics and Space Administration

The World Bank

Authors and Contributors

Alex Alusa	UNEP	Kenya
Gunilla Bjorklund	GeWa Consulting	Sweden
Gretchen C. Daily	Stanford University	USA
Till Darnhofer	UNEP	Austria
Ogunlade Davidson	University of Sierra Leone	Sierra Leone
Rodolfo Dirzo	UNAM	Mexico
John Dixon	The World Bank	USA
Ed Gómez	University of the Philippines	Philippines
Steven Hamburg	Brown University	USA
Anthony Janetos	NASA	USA
Calestous Juma	Convention on Biological Diversity	Kenya
Rhoda Krantz	Ecological Society of America	USA
Hoesung Lee	Korea Energy Economics Institute	Korea
Thomas Lovejoy	The World Bank	USA
Jane Lubchenco	Oregon State University	USA
Kathy Mackinnon	The World Bank	UK
Anthony McMichael	School of Hygiene & Tropical Medicine	UK
Jeff McNeely	IUCN	USA
Jerry Melillo	Ecosystem Research Center	USA
Harold Mooney	Stanford University	USA
Richard Moss	Battelle Pacific Northwest Laboratory	USA
Mohan Munasinghe	The World Bank	Sri Lanka
Nebojsa Nakicenovic	IIASA	Austria
Ian Noble	Australian National University	Australia
Richard Odingo	University of Nairobi	Kenya
Atiq Rahman	Bangladesh Centre for Advanced Studies	Bangladesh
Kilaparti Ramakrishna	The Woods Hole Research Centre	India
Walter Reid	World Resources Institute	USA
Manuel Rodríguez-Becerra	Intergovernmental Panel on Forestry	Colombia
Osvaldo Sala	University of Buenos Aires	Argentina
Setijati D. Sastrapadja	Centre for Biotechnology	Indonesia
Peter Schei	Directorate for Nature Management	Norway
Malena Sell	Brown University	Finland
Laura Van Wie McGrory	IPCC	USA
Pier Vellinga	Free University	The Netherlands
Robert Watson	The World Bank	USA
Hamdallah Zedan	UNEP	Egypt

TECHNICAL EDITORS
Laura Van Wie McGrory
Michael Keating

**COVER/BOOK DESIGN,
DESKTOP PUBLISHER**
Jim Cantrell

COPY EDITOR
Alison Raphael

Contents

BOXES

FIGURES

human beings and other living beings and the systems in which they exist.

Let us not forget that many of the human-induced changes in the global environment are qualitatively different from those seen before. As greater numbers of people require more food, more energy, and more goods and services, their requirements are in turn being reflected in global increases in fossil fuel combustion, agricultural production and associated use of land, fertilizers and pesticides, and increased utilization of freshwater resources. Increases in the severity of one major global environmental issue have the potential for exacerbating others. For instance, changes in the atmosphere and climate have effects that proliferate throughout the other global environmental issues. Increases in carbon dioxide concentrations will lead to changes in the amount and patterns of water use by individual species. A changed climate will lead to a loss of biodiversity as some species would no longer be able to cope with the new conditions. But it will also create opportunities for new species, weeds, and pests to multiply.

Unfortunately, efforts to achieve these goals are being implemented in ways that encourage a single-issue focus, setting the stage for implementation of measures that advance the attainment of one goal or objective at the expense of others. The single-issue and sectoral focus creates the potential for unproductive competition among environmental and development goals.

We have to develop technologies and practices that can simultaneously help meet important social and economic goals and also address interrelated environmental problems. One example is efforts to reduce greenhouse gas emissions through the use of modern plantation biomass energy—a practice that can have positive impacts on biodiversity, water quality, and land-management. Further, synergies can be achieved through carefully planned interventions that build on interlinkages among environmental issues.

This report, *Protecting Our Planet: Securing Our Future,* the result of a collaborative enterprise between the World Bank, U.S. National Aeronautics and Space Administration, and the United Nations Environment Programme, depicts in a comprehensive manner the linkages—physical and biochemical—between a number of environmental issues. It also addresses the means by which interlinked global environmental issues can be confronted in an integrated manner.

UNEP is pleased to have initiated and been associated with this study and recommends it to the wider environmental and policy community. I want to congratulate Robert Watson for his characteristic enthusiasm in making sure that the report comes out and thank my colleagues in the World Bank and NASA for their support.

This report would not have been possible without the many scientific and policy experts who contributed to it. Their contributions are acknowledged elsewhere in the report. My congratulations to all of them.

Klaus Töpfer
Executive Director
United Nations Environment Programme

Responses to global environmental issues are not fringe activities. They are central to meeting human needs and reducing poverty. This report recognizes a number of critical linkages among the global environment issues and meeting human needs. It also identifies a number of opportunities for strategic interventions. I wholeheartedly commit the Bank to do all it can to forge a global partnership to promote equitable approaches to global environmental issues, and to do so quickly. Time is not on our side. This agenda cannot afford to wait.

James D. Wolfensohn
President
The World Bank

Preface

THE GENESIS OF THIS REPORT was a United Nations Environment Programme (UNEP)-sponsored workshop on approaches to conserve and sustainably use biodiversity. At that meeting it was recognized that the scientific community, governments, and the secretariats of the global environmental conventions tended to view the issues of climate change, loss of biological diversity, land degradation/desertification, stratospheric ozone depletion, fresh and marine water degradation, deforestation/unsustainable forestry, and persistent organic pollutants in isolation. However, in reality these issues are closely connected.

At the conclusion of the workshop UNEP asked whether a small group of experts could be convened to prepare a brief report that identified the key scientific and policy linkages among these issues, and the linkages between these global environ-

mental issues and meeting the basic human needs of adequate food, clean water, energy and a healthy environment.

Policymakers who represent their governments at the international negotiating sessions of the environmental conventions are the intended audience for this work as well as the managers and planners in a wide variety of ministries, including agriculture, forestry, water resources, natural resource management, energy, and industry.

This document does not contain any original research but rather synthesizes information from a wide variety of international scientific and technical assessments and policy reports. It has been written by a small number of authors, and a much larger group of contributors, who are experienced in the scientific and policy aspects of these issues. The report represents the views and judgments of the individual authors and contributors and does not necessarily reflect the views of the three sponsoring agencies, UNEP, the U.S. National Aeronautics and Space Administration and the World Bank, or their governments.

This report has been made possible because of the dedication of a large number of people who have freely devoted their time to write, review, edit, and desktop it, often during their evenings and weekends. In particular I would like to acknowledge: the co-authors and contributors for their intellectual input, Laura Van Wie McGrory for technical editing, Jim Cantrell for desktop publishing and designing the cover and book, Lisa Segnestam for assisting with the figures, and Isabel Alegre for her tireless work in organizing meetings and teleconferences and ensuring that the co-authors and I stayed on schedule. In addition, many World Bank and UNEP staff contributed to this report by reviewing drafts and providing input to the Appendices.

I would also like to acknowledge the financial support from the United Nations Environment Programme (UNEP) and the U.S. National Aeronautics and Space Administration (NASA).

The fundamental conclusion of this report is that we must identify and understand the scientific and policy interlinkages among these issues and start to address them in a more holistic manner if the vision of sustainable development is to be realized.

Robert T. Watson
Director, Environment Department
The World Bank

Executive Summary

Protecting Our Planet — Securing Our Future
LINKAGES AMONG GLOBAL ENVIRONMENTAL ISSUES AND HUMAN NEEDS

The natural environment always has been exploited to fulfill human needs, but during this century the scale of our demands has grown so large that we are degrading the ecosystems upon which our health and livelihoods depend. However, socially and environmentally sustainable economic development can be realized by adopting an appropriate mix of technologies, policies, and practices that explicitly recognize the inextricable linkages among environmental systems and basic human needs.

MORE THAN TEN YEARS AFTER the Brundtland Commission[1] and six years after the Earth Summit in Rio, a number of global environmental problems are growing more severe and are beginning to threaten the ability of nations to meet the development goals of a growing human population. These global environmental problems include climate change, loss of biological diversity, land degradation and desertification, deforestation and forest degradation, pollution of fresh and marine waters, depletion of stratospheric ozone, and accumulation of persistent organic pollutants. Only in the case of ozone depletion have nations taken significant steps to reverse the decline. The composition of the atmosphere, the availability and quality of fresh water, the productivity of agricultural land, and the structure and functioning of terrestrial and marine ecosystems are changing as a result of human activities. These changes are occurring at unprecedented rates, and in some cases are qualitatively different than changes seen before. The Earth currently is approaching the point where its physical and biological systems may not be able to meet human demands for environmental goods and services, threatening the ability of nations to meet their populations' basic needs for adequate food and clean water, energy supplies, safe shelter, and a healthy environment. In some regions of the world, this point already has been reached. Governments and other sectors of society have acknowledged, in Agenda 21 and a series of international conventions and agreements, that global environmental protection and sustainable economic development are inextricably linked: Each depends on the other.

The Earth's physical and biological systems (land, atmosphere, and oceans) provide humans with the goods and services essential for survival and good health. These include goods such as food, timber, and medicines; and services such as the purification of air and water, soil generation and maintenance of soil fertility, pollination of crops and natural vegetation, dispersal of seeds, preservation of biodiversity, and control of the vast majority of agricultural pests. The Earth's natural systems also stabilize the Earth's climate, offer protection from the sun's harmful ultraviolet rays, and provide aesthetic beauty and support for the world's diverse cultures.

Global environmental problems and the ability to meet human needs are linked through a set of physical, chemical, and biological processes. The major components of the Earth system—its biogeochemical cycles, the climate system, and the protective ozone layer—all interact to regulate the composition of the atmosphere, the productivity of oceans and land, and the sustainability of ecosystem goods and services. When human activities affect one component of the Earth system, there often are ramifications for other components as well. For example, a change in the Earth's climate would likely reduce biodiversity, change the distribution and productivity of forests, and increase the rate of loss of stratospheric ozone. Likewise, conversion of forests to other types of land cover can increase greenhouse gas emissions into the atmosphere and thus contribute to change climate, and can reduce biological diversity and affect water resources.

Actions taken to fulfill human needs are increasingly recognized to have local, regional, and global environmental consequences. Global environmental problems and the ability to meet human needs are linked through local, regional, and global patterns of natural resource degradation and air and water pollution. Recognizing these links provides policymakers with an excellent opportunity to cost-effectively address global environmental issues at the local, national, and regional levels. Multiple environmental and development goals can be achieved by adopting a combination of technologies, policies, and measures that explicitly recognize the linkages among the environmental problems and satisfying human needs.

All global environmental problems are caused by the same underlying driving forces: population size, level of consumption, and choice of technologies. Demand for environmental goods and services depends on the size of populations and people's desire to obtain basic goods and increase standards of living. The ways in which these needs and desires are fulfilled depend on a society's choice of technologies, which in turn have a large influence on global, regional, and local environmental change. The burden of responsibility for the impacts of these choices varies widely. All people affect the environment, but richer people (and thus richer nations) have a disproportionate impact due to higher per capita levels of resource consumption and pollution. Poor communities, however, typically are the most vulnerable to the effects of environmental degradation, since they have fewer resources for adapting to and resolving environmental problems. Widespread poverty and inequity are aggravated by environmental decline, and also can exacerbate environmental degradation when poor communities are compelled to overexploit local resources to survive.

Addressing global environmental issues in an integrated manner can be accomplished using many of the same technologies and policy instruments that are used to contend with the issues separately, but in different combinations. Because of the links among the global environmental problems and the resources needed to meet human needs, chosen technologies and policies will rarely maximize any individual outcome. Nevertheless, recognition of these linkages offers the opportunity to identify cost-effective interventions that yield multiple benefits ("win-win" options) and advance progress toward a more sustainable future. Such progress can be achieved by incorporating awareness of global environmental issues into all sectoral decisions, including management of agriculture, forestry, energy, and water resources; and efforts to correct market, policy, institutional, and knowledge failures. "Command and control" policies, market mechanisms, and voluntary agreements, used in various combinations, can help bring about such changes. Governments can encourage this process by creating an enabling policy environment, establishing a supporting regulatory framework, mobilizing public involvement, and fostering civil institutions to address these issues.

Achieving a sustainable world will require improved institutional arrangements—involving governments, the private sector, nonprofit organizations, and academia—at the national, regional, and global levels. Important progress can be made through the formation of new partnerships among key actors that build upon their comparative advantages, and by overcoming the fragmented, sectoral decision structures of both national and international institutions and organizations. Significant potential also exists to improve integration of scientific input into the existing environmental conventions, through the preparation of scientific assessments that meet the needs of multiple institutions and agreements.

The current rate of global environmental degradation is unprecedented, and there is potential for surprises and non-linearities. Time scales associated with reversing environmental damage often are on the order of decades to centuries, and some damages—e.g., species loss—are irreversible. Adequate time to address these issues is a luxury that may not always be available. The implications of current rates of resource depletion and environmental degradation—the undermining of the very foundation of long-term sustainable economic development—warrant consideration of a more precautionary approach to environmental policy formulation.

Note

1. The 1987 UN World Commission on Environment and Development (the "Brundtland Commission"), stated that sustainable development "...meets the needs of the present without compromising the ability of future generations to meet their needs."

W here there are threats of serious or irreversible damage, scientific uncertainty shall not be used to postpone cost-effective measures to prevent environmental degradation."

— Rio Declaration on Environment and Development

Part I

INTRODUCTION

THE IMPORTANCE OF GLOBAL environmental issues—such as climate change, loss of biological diversity, stratospheric ozone depletion, deforestation, and water degradation—to poverty alleviation and development is now becoming more fully recognized. However, these global environmental issues are, to a large extent, normally thought of as isolated issues by both the scientific and policy communities. As a result, they often fail to adequately recognize that there are strong scientific and policy interlinkages among the global environmental issues, between global environmental issues and local and regional environmental issues, and between environmental issues and basic human needs—adequate food, clean water, energy services, and a healthy environment. If these global environmental issues are to be addressed within a more holistic and synergistic policy framework, it is essential to gain an improved understanding of the scientific and policy interlinkages among them and how they influence our ability to meet basic human needs.

THE CHALLENGE OF MEETING HUMAN NEEDS

One of the major challenges facing humankind is to provide an equitable standard of living for this and future generations: adequate food, clean water and energy, safe shelter, a healthy environment, an educated public, and satisfying work. Today more than 1.3 billion people live on less than $1 per day and 3 billion people live on less than $2 per day, 800 million people are malnourished, 1.3 billion people live without clean water, 2 billion people live without sanitation, 2 billion people lack electricity, and 1.4 billion people are ex-

Poverty often means inadequate housing and lack of access to clean water and sanitation services.

posed to dangerous levels of outdoor air pollution. These unfulfilled needs for a clean and healthy environment cause millions of people to die prematurely each year.

Over the next century the world's population is expected to double. To meet the needs of this growing population while significantly reducing the number of people in abject poverty implies a number of formidable development challenges:

- Double food production within the next 35 years without further conversion of critical natural habitats and excessive use of chemicals
- Provide clean water and sanitation to everyone
- Provide the energy services needed to stimulate economic growth without continued degradation of land, air, and water
- Develop safe urban environments without excessive air and water pollution
- Improve health care facilities
- Provide educational opportunities, especially for girls
- Provide countries with assistance so that they can access, generate, disseminate, and utilize the knowledge required to develop in a socially and environmentally sustainable manner.

SUSTAINABLE DEVELOPMENT DEPENDS ON A HEALTHY ENVIRONMENT

Our economic systems, our health, and our lifestyles depend on the continued adequate functioning of ecological systems. In very broad terms, the availability of natural goods and services is controlled by the hydrologic cycle, biogeochemical cycles, the climate system, and the maintenance of biological diversity and functioning ecosystems.

The Earth's natural ecosystems—living organisms interacting with each other and their physical environment—provide humans with a vast array of marketable ecosystem goods, such as seafood, forage, timber, biomass fuels, natural fibers, and many pharmaceuticals, industrial products and their precursors. These natural ecosystem goods are in addition to the major products from managed ecosystems, such as the output from agriculture, aquaculture, livestock, and plantation forestry. The harvest and trade of ecosystem goods represent an essential and familiar part of the human economy.

Ecosystems also provide services that typically are not traded in the marketplace, but are fundamental parts of our life-support system. Those ecosystem services include:

- Purification of air and water
- Detoxification and decomposition of wastes
- Stabilization and moderation of the Earth's climate
- Moderation of floods and droughts
- Moderation of temperature extremes and the force of winds and waves
- Generation and renewal of soil and soil fertility

- Dispersal of seeds
- Pollination of plants, including crops
- Control of pests
- Maintenance of biodiversity, including genetic diversity, from which humanity derives key inputs to its agricultural, medicinal, and industrial enterprise
- Support of diverse human cultures and provision of aesthetic beauty.

THE RATE OF CHANGE IS GROWING

For millennia, human demands on the planet's ecosystems have been growing steadily, in some cases gradually overloading local and regional ecosystems. Deforestation and faulty irrigation practices in the Middle East caused land degradation as early as 7,000 years ago, and the resulting decline in food production led to the decline of whole societies. Plato wrote, in the fifth century BC, that deforestation and erosion were wasting away the land. For centuries, deforestation and land degradation were regional problems, undermining societies in many parts of the world.

By the middle of this century—with a growing world population and rising per capita consumption driven by increasing affluence and choice of technologies—human impacts on the environment had become global in scale. As the demand for food, clean water, and energy services has increased, the ability of the environment to meet some of these needs has been threatened (see box A). Examples of this degradation include unprecedented changes in the composition of the atmosphere, the amount of high quality fresh water, the productivity of the land, and the structure and functioning of terrestrial and marine ecosystems.

Many of these human-induced changes in the global environment are qualitatively different from

Power generation, essential for economic development, may cause local and global environmental damage.

Box A

Underlying reasons for environmental degradation

- Increased demand for water, biological resources, and energy services as a result of economic and population growth
- Failure of governments to regulate the use of water, biological resources, and energy for sustainable development, which will require a transition to viewing many of these resources more as economic than public goods
- Choice of inappropriate technologies
- Failure to internalize environmental externalities into market prices, that is, appropriately reflect the costs of environmental degradation in market prices
- Failure of markets and governments in their national income accounting to recognize the true value of natural resources (e.g., water and biological resources)
- Failure to appropriate the regional and global economic values of natural resources and ecological services to the local level
- Failure to consider the long-term consequences of development activities.

those seen before. For example, the production, use, and discarding of chemicals that have never before existed, such as insecticides, herbicides, chlorofluorocarbons, and halons have had completely unanticipated effects, such as the destruction of stratospheric ozone by chlorofluorocarbons and halons. Conversely, while other environmental impacts of modern society are not qualitatively different from those seen before, their magnitude and rates of change produce dramatically new phenomena. Since 1850 energy consumption (see figure 1) and agricultural production have increased dramatically. These trends are leading to changes in atmospheric concentrations of carbon dioxide, a key greenhouse gas, well outside the range of natural variation over the last several hundred thousand years (see figure 2). Although more by accident than by design, humans now influence conditions over the entire biosphere.

Our growing use of the environment is beginning to exceed the assimilative and regenerative capacities of Earth's major biological and physical systems, both regionally and globally. The Earth may be approaching a point where it will not be able to meet the demand for environmental goods and services. These changes are beginning to have adverse consequences for human populations, especially the poorest segments of society.

DRIVING FORCES OF ENVIRONMENTAL CHANGE

The scale of human impact on the environment is determined by three interdependent factors, which can be called the driving forces of environmental change. They are the size of the human population, the per capita consumption of resources (which is usually related to the affluence of a society), and the technologies used to produce and consume these resources.

FIGURE 1

Global primary energy consumption by source, and total in EJ/yr, 1860–1990
(data for crude oil include non-energy feedstocks)

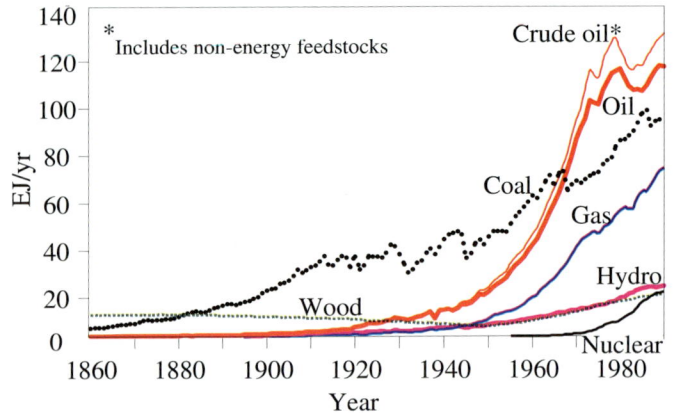

Sources: IPCC, 1996 (WG2 Energy Primer); BP, various volumes; IEA, 1993; Marchetti and Nakicenovic, 1979.

The global human population, after millions of years of slow increase, began to grow rapidly about two centuries ago. During this century alone the global population has grown from about 1.6 bil-

FIGURE 2

Global temperatures and atmospheric carbon dioxide

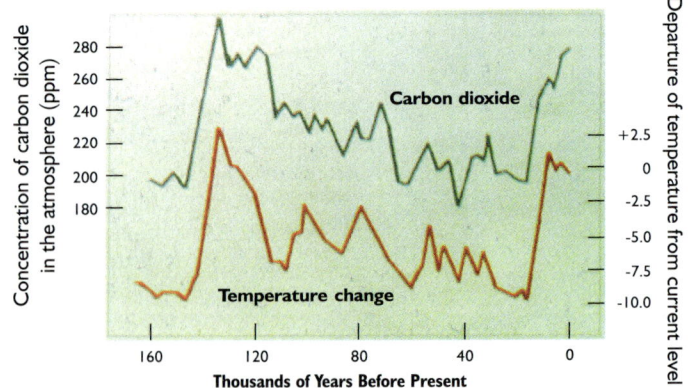

Source: Office of Science and Technology Policy. Washington, D.C.

lion to nearly 6 billion. Mid-range population projections from the United Nations forecast a world population of close to 10 billion within 50 years, given current trends (see figure 3). Any growth in population brings at least some increased environmental pressures, as people consume food, use energy, seek fresh water and sanitation, build homes, and seek productive jobs.

Hence the issue of population growth is very important. The population conference in Cairo in 1994 recognized that reducing the rate of population growth is closely linked to economic development. The delegates recognized that there should be three elements in any successful program to limit population growth: culturally acceptable forms of contraception, education of girls and women, and microenterprise lending to women. The empowerment of women will be absolutely critical in limiting population growth, hence in dealing with environmental issues.

FIGURE 3

Projected population of the world, 1990–2150

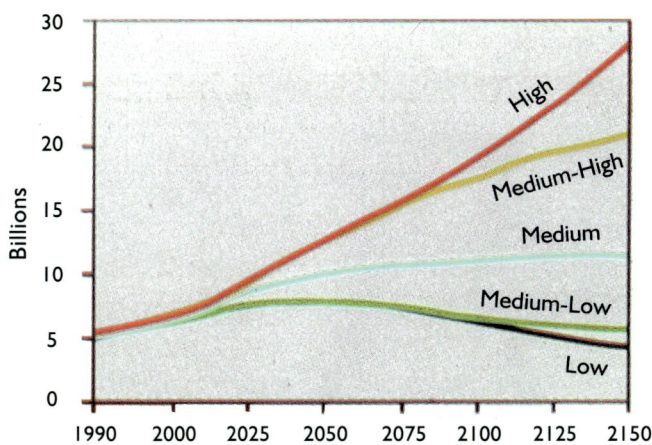

Source: United Nations Population Division, Long-Range Populations Projections, Two Centuries of Population Growth, 1990–2150. United Nations, New York.

The magnitude of the environmental impact of human societies depends on the form of consumption; and consumption, particularly in the richer nations, has been increasing at a faster rate than the global population. Since 1900 the world's population has more than tripled, while the global economy has grown 20-fold, fossil fuel consumption 30-fold, and industrial activity 50-fold. Annual world consumption of all forms of commercially sold energy is now the equivalent of 26,000 supertankers, each carrying two million barrels of oil. Most of the economic development has happened since 1950 in the two dozen richest countries—most of them in the Northern Hemisphere. These countries contain less than one quarter of the world's population, but they are responsible for more than half of the annual consumption of a number of resources, including commercially sold energy, metal, and wood. Through their use of fossil energy, the rich countries also emit the bulk of greenhouse gases, such as carbon dioxide.

Technology, from the harnessing of fire to the development of computers, has allowed the human population to expand while living in ever greater comfort and security. Technology allows us to reshape our environment by actively paving the land, damming rivers, clearing forests, and—as a by-product of our activities—changing the composition of the atmosphere. It is our choice of technologies that determines the magnitude of many environmental impacts. The wise and effective use of technologies will be essential if we are going to provide goods and services for a growing population while reducing the environmental impact on a per person basis. However, there are limits to what technology can do. Recycling reduces waste but does not eliminate it. Using cleaner and more energy-efficient machines results in less pollution per machine, but if we buy more of them and use them more often, the gains are eroded. Finally, technologies will only work if we choose to employ them.

Cultural, social, and economic forces and institutions also influence these three basic factors driving environmental change and the interactions among them. Whether these are religious beliefs, political rights, or the functioning of economic markets, these forces clearly and dramatically influence the environmental impact of any specific technology.

RECOGNIZING THE THREAT

It has taken humanity a very long time to begin to realize the scope and scale of environmental changes. One of the important reasons for this failing is that we take ecosystem functioning and services for granted. Because there is no "price" for breathable air, it is considered to be a free good. Because ecosystem services are not normally traded in the marketplace, there are no market mechanisms in place to alert society to their rapidly declining status. The widespread ecological and human health costs of releasing pollutants into the general environment are not normally counted in the balance sheets of companies or the national accounts of governments. Therefore, they are called "externalities." Only in recent years have some organizations begun to try to subtract ecosystem and human health losses from balance sheets in an effort to give a truer picture of the economic state of our societies.

The international scientific, environmental, and policy communities have begun to recognize the seriousness of such worldwide environmental issues as climate change, the depletion of the stratospheric ozone layer, the loss of biological diversity, desertification and land degradation, unsustainable use of forests, degradation of freshwater and marine resources, and the accumulation of persistent organic pollutants (see box B). While some of these, such as climate change and damage to the ozone layer, have emerged as truly global issues, their impact is

---

Box B

Evolution of major international global environmental conferences and agreements

1972 Stockholm Conference on the Human Environment
1982 Law of the Sea
1985 Vienna Convention for the Protection of the Ozone Layer
1987 Montreal Protocol on Substances that Deplete the Ozone Layer (later strengthened in a series of amendments and adjustments)
1992 The UN Conference on Environment and Development
- Agenda 21 and the Rio Declaration
- Convention on Biological Diversity
- Convention on Climate Change
- Statement of Principles on Forest Management, Conservation and Sustainable Development
1994 The UN Convention to Combat Desertification
1995 Global Programme for Action for the Protection of the Marine Environment from Land-based Activities
1997 Kyoto Protocol on Greenhouse Gases
1997 The UN Convention on the Law of the Non-Navigational Uses of International Watercourses
1998 Convention on the Prior Informed Consent (PIC) Procedure for Certain Hazardous Chemicals and Pesticides in International Trade

felt at the local and regional levels, for example, agricultural productivity and availability of water. The others are more directly linked to the more familiar long-standing local, national, and regional environmental issues of air and water pollution and soil degradation.

International environmental conventions have been negotiated for four of these issues (climate change, stratospheric ozone depletion, loss of biological diversity, and desertification). However, these global environmental issues are, to a large extent, thought of as isolated issues by both the scientific and policy communities, which have failed to adequately recognize the strong scientific and policy linkages:

The United Nations has been the leader in developing consensus on global environmental concerns.

■ *Among global environmental issues.* For example, changes in climate can change the structure and functioning of ecological systems, which in turn can affect the Earth's climate by altering the emissions of key greenhouse gases from ecological systems.

■ *Between global environmental issues and local and regional environmental issues.* For example, the combustion of coal results in local air pollution (fine particulates and oxidants), regional air pollution (acid and heavy metal deposition), and climate change. In turn, changes in climate can increase the levels of local air pollutants such as ozone.

■ *Between environmental issues and human needs.* For example, agricultural practices affect climate through emissions of greenhouse gases, while climate changes affect our ability to produce food.

While considerable progress has been made in addressing local air and water quality issues in some places, progress on protecting the global environment since the Earth Summit in Rio has been limited. Atmospheric concentrations of greenhouse gases have continued to increase by about one percent per year. Natural habitats continue to be lost at increasing rates; wetlands and forests are now disappearing at a rate of about one half to one percent each year. Freshwater continues to be degraded. The major bright spot is that the concentrations of a number of ozone-depleting substances have stopped increasing in the atmosphere, and some have even decreased as a result of the Vienna Convention to Protect the Ozone Layer and the associated Montreal Protocol (see figure 4).

We face a daunting set of challenges: meeting both social and environmental goals in the face of rapid population and economic growth. Rising to these challenges will require societies to become far more efficient in the use of energy and natural resources. Success in dealing with global environmental problems will in large part determine our ability to meet our goals for sustainable development. For example, projected changes in climate, loss of biological diversity, and desertification all

FIGURE 4

Ozone-depleting chemicals have begun to decrease in the lower atmosphere

Atmospheric abundance of ozone-depleting chemicals from humans (chlorine and bromine as "equivalent chlorine" in the troposphere, ppb).

Since 1994, the amount of these chemicals present in the atmosphere has decreased.

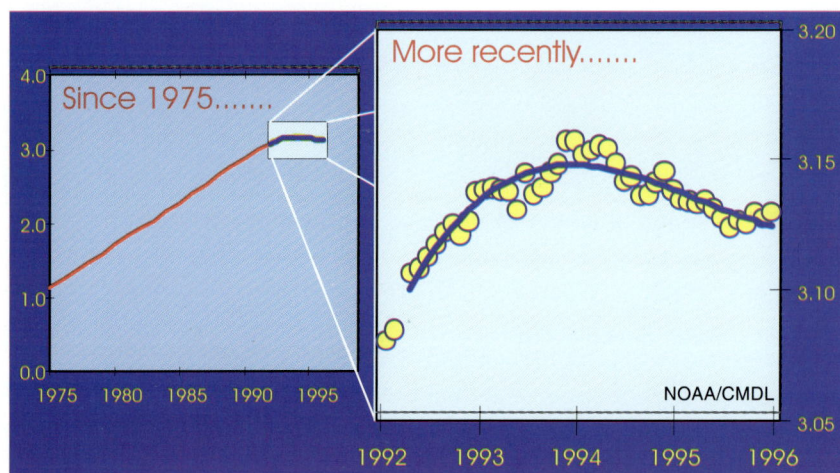

Use of CFCs, HCFCs, chlorinated solvents, and halons caused a dramatic increase in the atmospheric abundance of chemicals (chlorine and bromine) capable of depleting stratospheric ozone in the years before 1994.

Note: For additional information see, http://www.cmdl.noaa.gov/noah/totalcl/totalcl.html.
Source: Montzka et al. 1996. *Science,* 272, 1318-1322.

threaten water resources and the sustainability of world food production. This is occurring at a time when the demand for water and food is rapidly increasing because of economic development and population growth, thus placing severe demands on water resource management and agricultural productivity.

A successful transition to development that is economically, socially, and environmentally sound and sustainable over the long term will entail a series of important changes.

One such change is to foster a clear and widespread recognition of the fundamental linkages between environmental quality and sustainable development. It is important for both governments and industries to recognize that there is no ultimate dichotomy between sustainable economic growth and environmental protection, and that the environment cannot be viewed as a luxury yet to be afforded. The reason for protecting the environment is not merely to help the economy perform better. Rather, it is that the natural environment is the ultimate source of all material inputs and services upon which the world's economy depends. True environmental protection means moving to more ecologically sound forms of energy generation and food production, to eco-efficient industries, and to lifestyles that recognize natural limits.

Win-win, cost-effective solutions can reduce environmental impacts while meeting immediate and long-term human needs. For example, modern renewable energy technologies are often cost-competitive, particularly in many rural areas, and can avoid the environmental damages caused by the combustion of fossil fuels. It is equally important to avoid win-lose actions that address one global environmental issue, but cause another problem. An inappropriately designed large dam could displace the use of fossil fuels, but might also cause significant loss of biodiversity, harmful changes in water flows, and the displacement of valley dwellers, perhaps without adequate resettlement plans.

Sustainable development will require correcting market, policy, institutional, and knowledge failures. It also will require a major change in the understanding and attitudes of many people along with the development of fundamentally new ways of accounting for the environment as an economic good and reflecting this in national accounts. Environmentally sound market behavior can be stimulated through the creation of an enabling policy environment and an appropriate national and international regulatory framework. The success of such efforts will depend on the empowerment of citizens and local communities to participate in decision-making; the creation of partnerships between governments, the private sector, development agencies and non-profit organizations; the development and widespread sharing of knowledge; investments in environmentally compatible techniques, products and processes; and the mobilization of financial resources for development.

A prerequisite to making true progress toward a sustainable world for all people is the recognition that meeting several goals at one time will usually prevent us from maximizing any single objective. For example, the approaches that maximize agricultural output may significantly diminish water quality and biodiversity and thus the long-term basis for resilient food production; or land-use policies that maximize the quantity of land protected for biodiversity may reduce agricultural outputs. If we are to meet our many goals we cannot consider them in isolation; they must be viewed as interdependent and interlinked. This multiple-factor approach provides our only hope of real progress toward an equitable and sustainable future. It also provides us with our biggest challenge.

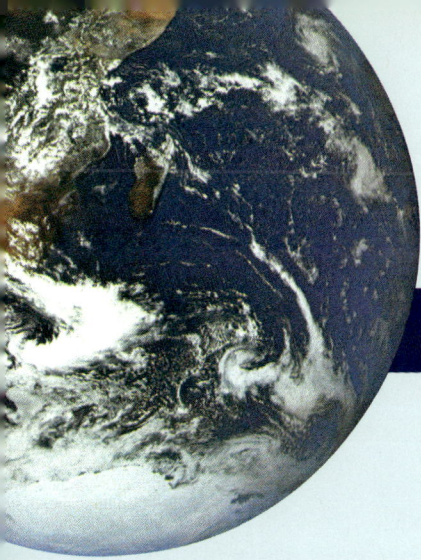

Part II

GLOBAL ENVIRONMENTAL ISSUES

THE MAJOR GLOBAL ENVIRON- mental issues can be divided into two categories: those involving the global commons and those of worldwide importance, but not directly involving the global commons. Global commons issues involve major components of the Earth system (see box C), such as the atmosphere, oceans, and land surface, and can be effectively addressed only if all societies are involved. Climate change, ozone layer depletion, marine pollution, and the build-up of persistent organic pollutants in the environment are global commons issues because releases into the atmosphere or the oceans, independently of where they occur, cause global changes in the Earth's biophysical systems. Mitigation of global commons issues thus can only be accomplished through coordinated actions among nations. Issues of worldwide importance include loss of biological diversity, desertification and land degradation, degradation of fresh waters, and deforestation and unsustainable use of forests. As these local and regional problems grow in scope and scale, they will have serious cumulative impacts on the planetary life-support system. These issues can be effectively addressed on a regional basis, but often require multilateral agreements, such as agreements to combat acid rain in Europe, desertification in Africa, and pollution of regional seas. Appendix 2 provides concise descriptions of each of the global environmental issues.

STATE OF SCIENTIFIC KNOWLEDGE OF GLOBAL ENVIRONMENTAL CHANGES

Climate change

Human activities, primarily the burning of fossil fuels such as coal, oil and natural gas,

Box C

Major components of the Earth system

The Earth's atmosphere: The Earth's weather, climate, and stratospheric ozone layer are controlled by the interplay among physical, chemical, biological, and ecological processes. It is the interactions among these processes that determine the weather at any place and time. Changes in one part of the system affect all other parts of the system, though not necessarily in a linear or easily predictable manner.

Bretherton Diagram

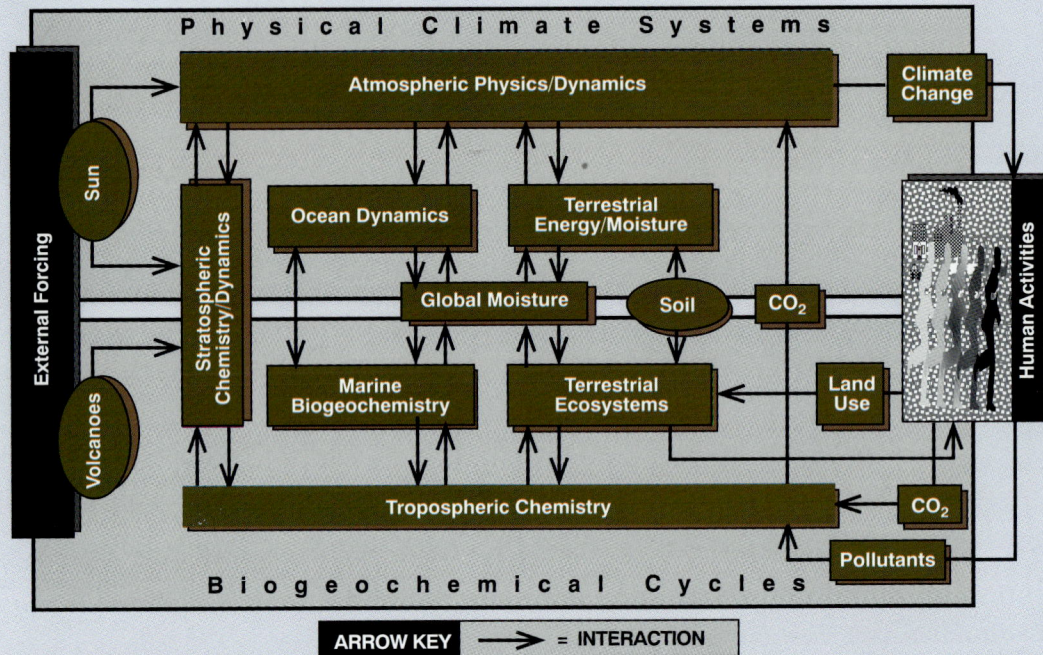

Source: NASA, 1986. *Earth Systems Science Overview: A Program for Global Change.* Washington, DC.

The Earth's climate: Ultraviolet and visible radiation from the sun heat the Earth's surface, causing infra-red radiation to be emitted back out to space and water vapor to be evaporated from land and ocean surfaces. This solar heating is amplified by greenhouse gases in the atmosphere, primarily water vapor and carbon dioxide, which trap some of the outgoing infra-red radiation and re-radiate some of it back to the Earth's surface. Thus the greenhouse gases act as a thermal blanket, causing the Earth to be $35^{\circ}C$ warmer than it would be in their absence. Seasonal and latitudinal variations in the amount of sunlight reaching the Earth's surface, combined with the Earth's rotation, produce the major oceanic and atmospheric circulation patterns, which are responsible for local weather and seasonal changes in climate. Ocean circulation strongly influences climate and weather on multiple time scales. Biological and ecological processes play an important role in modulating the Earth's climate at both the regional and global scale by controlling the amounts of water vapor and other greenhouse gases that enter the atmosphere. Regional climate is strongly influenced by terrestrial ecosystems because plant transpiration influences the amount of water vapor entering the atmosphere, while global climate is partly controlled by the fluxes of carbon dioxide, nitrous oxide, and methane from ecological systems. The Earth's climate is now changing on the regional and global scale because human activities are changing the rates at which water and other greenhouse gases enter the atmosphere.

Box C — Major components of the Earth system *(continued)*

The Earth's protective ozone layer: Ultraviolet radiation from the sun produces ozone in the Earth's upper atmosphere by breaking apart oxygen molecules in the stratosphere. The amount of stratospheric ozone, in the absence of human activities, is controlled by the abundance of a variety of chemicals that are produced by physical, biological, and ecological processes in the oceans and on land and transported into the upper atmosphere by atmospheric circulation patterns. The ozone layer absorbs damaging ultraviolet radiation, thus protecting humans and ecological systems. Human activities have depleted the Earth's ozone layer by about 5 percent due to the release of ozone-depleting gases, such as chlorofluorocarbons, into the atmosphere.

The Earth's biogeochemical systems: Living organisms play an important role in regulating the cycling of chemicals on Earth. Plants convert atmospheric carbon dioxide to biologically usable forms of carbon through photosynthesis. Nitrogen in the air is converted to biologically usable forms by the activity of microbes, which exist in part in symbiotic relationships with higher plants. Carbon and nitrogen are cycled by organisms through the processes of growth, death, and decomposition. Bacteria, fungi, and other organisms are responsible for decomposition in the Earth's oceans and soils. Analogous processes control the fluxes of other chemical constituents of the Earth system. Thus, while non-organic geochemical processes, such as the weathering of rocks, are responsible for the presence of many chemicals in the Earth's environment, living processes are responsible for their cycling. Disturbance of these biogeochemical cycles can have profound effects on the patterns of life on Earth.

The Earth's biological systems: Estimates of the total number of species vary widely; the Global Biodiversity Assessment concluded that there are likely about 13 million species, of which only about one-tenth have been identified. These species interact through competition for resources, and in symbiotic, predator-prey, and parasitic relationships. Biological diversity at all levels (ecosystems, species, populations, and genes) plays an important role in the response of ecosystems to environmental stress; for example, reductions of biodiversity below natural ranges may result in decreased resilience of ecosystems. The wealth of biological interactions and populations' responses to each other and to the physical environment constitute the raw material for evolutionary change in both the short and long terms. The Earth's biological systems are comprised of a series of linked components. Changes in one component, such as tropical forests, open oceans, or temperate wetlands, will influence the functioning of the system as a whole. A wide variety of organisms are responsible for the pattern of resources that humans use, including freshwater, food, timber, and energy. Understanding fully the impacts of any resource management decision, therefore, depends on acknowledging the interactions among the Earth's biophysical systems.

and land-use practices, particularly deforestation, are changing the atmospheric concentrations of greenhouse gases that shape our planet's climate. The amount of heat-trapping carbon (in the form of carbon dioxide) released each year by human activities is estimated at 6 billion tons of carbon from burning fossil fuels and 1 to 2 billion tons from land-use changes, including deforestation. Of this 7 to 8 billion tons, the oceans absorb about 2 billion tons of carbon a year, and plant growth globally absorbs another 1.5 to 2.5 billion tons, resulting in a net addition of about 3.5 billion tons of carbon to the atmosphere each year. Humans already have increased the levels of carbon dioxide in the atmosphere by more than 30 percent since the beginning of the industrial revolution and the large-scale use of fossil fuels.

The Earth's climate has warmed by about one-half degree Centigrade this century (see figure 5). The weight of scientific evidence suggests that human activities have contributed to this trend. The climate is projected to warm another 1 to 3.5 degrees Centigrade over the next century due to projected increases in atmospheric concentrations

FIGURE 5

Global observed temperatures

Combined global land, air, and sea surface temperatures 1860 to August 1998 (relative to 1961–1990 average)

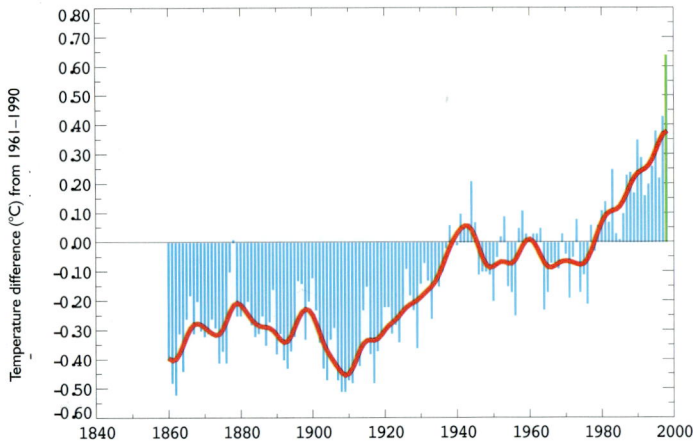

Source: The U.K. Meteorological Office. 1997. *Climate Change and Its Impacts: A Global Perspective.* Brittanic Crown Copyright.

of greenhouse gases (see figure 6). This would be a faster rate of warming than any observed during the last 10,000 years. The projected temperature changes will be accompanied by changes in the amount and patterns of precipitation, leading, in many areas, to more floods and droughts. It will also be accompanied by a rise in sea level of 15 to 95 centimeters.

While these human-influenced changes in the global climate are likely to benefit some regions (by increasing agricultural productivity at high latitudes), they will also cause serious problems in many parts of the world, including:

- Significant increases in the geographic range and incidence of insect-borne diseases, particularly malaria and dengue, in the tropics and sub-tropics
- Increased risk of hunger and famine for many of the world's poorest people who depend on isolated agricultural systems, especially in the tropics and sub-tropics

- The displacement by rising sea levels of tens of millions of people from small island states and the low-lying delta areas of Egypt, Bangladesh, and China (see figure 7)
- Shifts in the distribution, structure, and functioning of terrestrial and aquatic ecosystems, and potentially irreversible changes, such as loss of biodiversity
- Decreased amounts of precipitation in many arid and semi-arid areas.

These changes will directly and indirectly affect human welfare. Populations in developing countries are generally more vulnerable than those in developed countries, which are the source of most carbon emissions. Estimates of total economic damage from a 2 to 3°C warming tend to be a few percent of world GDP, with considerably higher levels of damage to developing countries. These estimates include both potential negative and positive effects, but are highly uncertain because many effects—such as non-market damages to ecosystem services—are

FIGURE 6

Projected temperatures

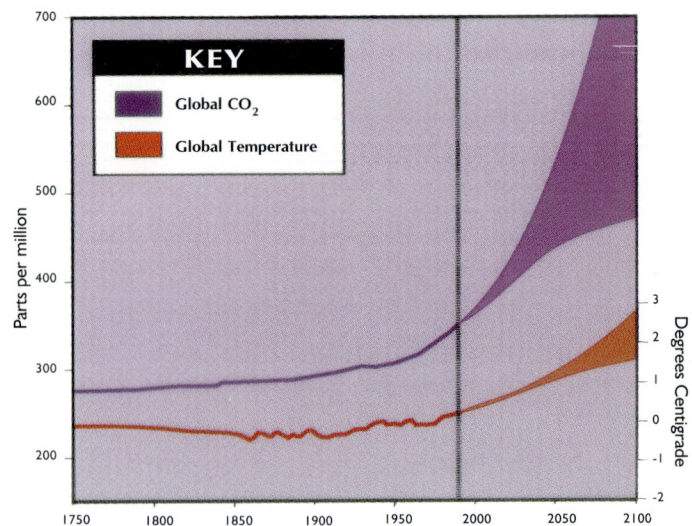

Source: IPCC. 1995. *Second Assessment Report. Working Group 1.* Cambridge.

FIGURE 7

Land at risk in a delta — Potential losses in Bangladesh due to a 1m rise in sea level

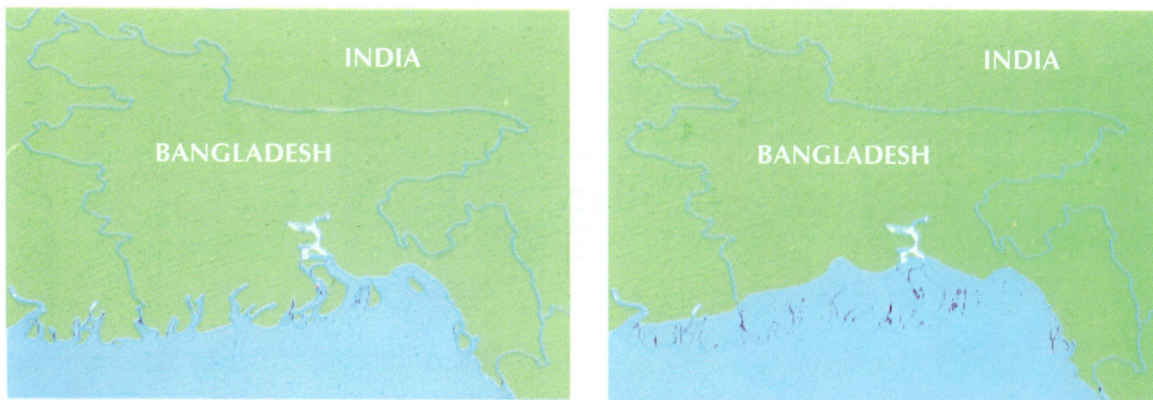

Source: World Bank.

difficult to quantify. In addition, the relationship between the beneficial effects of CO_2 fertilization and the negative effects of increases in agricultural pests and increased climatic variability is uncertain.

The sensitivity of both natural and managed systems to climate variation is illustrated by the effects of fluctuations of a "normal" climate. El Niño, a periodic natural shift in temperatures in the Pacific Ocean, caused a serious disruption in global weather patterns in 1998. These disruptions resulted in devastating fires in Southeast Asia (particularly Indonesia), the Amazon, southern Mexico, Florida, Greece and western Canada, and severe flooding in numerous regions, notably northern China.

Stratospheric ozone depletion

Stratospheric ozone, which protects life on Earth from much of the sun's harmful ultraviolet-B radiation, has been depleted at all latitudes except the tropics and sub-tropics as a result of emissions of human-created compounds (see figure 8). The chemicals involved, including chlorofluorocarbons (CFCs), halons, and related substances, have been used for decades in refrigerators and air-condition-

ers, and as cleaning solvents, foam blowing agents, aerosol propellants, and fire extinguishing agents. In the stratospheric ozone layer, 15 to 50 kilometers above the surface of the Earth, these long-lived chlorine- and bromine-containing substances are decomposed by sunlight and chemically react to destroy ozone molecules.

Ozone depletion is greatest in the polar regions in late winter and early spring. Since 1979 the ozone layer at northern mid-latitudes (30-60°) has decreased by about 6 percent in winter and spring, and 3 percent in summer and fall. It has decreased by about 5 percent at southern mid-latitudes on a year-round basis. This depletion has resulted in an increase in the level of UV-B radiation reaching the Earth's surface. Each 1 percent depletion in the amount of ozone overhead results in just over a 1 percent increase in UV-B at ground level.

A sustained increase in ground-level UV-B radiation has a number of harmful effects, including:

■   A significant increase in the incidence of melanoma and non-melanoma skin cancer in light-skinned people

15

FIGURE 8
Arctic ozone image time series, 1979–97

The satellite images show significant ozone depletion in the 1990s relative to the the 1980s.

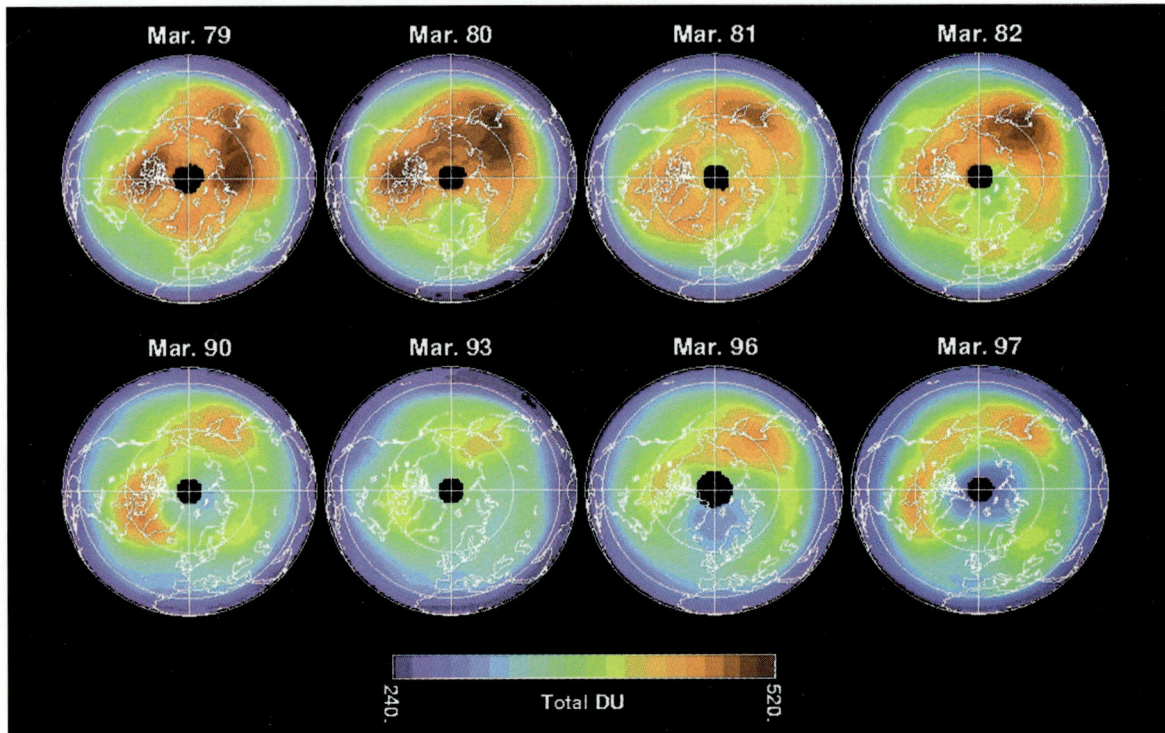

Source: Paul Newman/NASA Goddard Space Flight Center. 1997.

- An accelerated formation of eye cataracts, which are the leading cause of blindness in many developing countries
- Potential suppression of the human immune system
- A decrease in the productivity of some terrestrial and aquatic ecological systems
- A decrease in air quality, because UV-B radiation reacts with a number of air pollutants to form harmful oxidants, including tropospheric ozone.

Because of the effectiveness of the Montreal Protocol and subsequent amendments and adjustments, stratospheric ozone levels are projected to stop declining within the next decade or two, then slowly increase to pre-1970 levels in the middle of the next century. These projections assume full compliance with the latest international agreements on control measures reached in Montreal in 1997.

Loss of biological diversity

Biological diversity, or biodiversity, refers to the variety of life on Earth, including the variety of species, the genetic variability within each species, and the variety of different ecosystems. The Earth's biodiversity is a result of hundreds of millions of years of evolution of life on this planet.

Human activities are causing a loss of biological diversity among animals and plants globally estimated at 50 to 100 times the average rate of species loss that would be expected in the absence of human activities. The two most species-rich biomes are tropical forests and coral reefs. Tropical forests are under threat largely from conversion to other land-uses, while coral reefs are experiencing increasing levels of overexploitation and pollution. If current rates of loss of tropical forests continue for the next 30 years (about 1 percent per year), the projected number of species that the remaining forest could support would be reduced by 5 to 10 percent relative to the forest in the absence of human disturbance. This rate of decline would represent 1,000 to 10,000 times the expected rate of extinction without deforestation by humans.

Some studies suggest that, globally, as many as one-half of all mammal and bird species may become extinct within 200 to 300 years, and that the projected rate of extinction of species may equal that of the rapid extinction of the dinosaurs 65 million years ago.

Biodiversity loss can result from a number of activities, including:

- Habitat conversion and destruction
- Fragmentation of large ecosystems into smaller, disconnected patches of original vegetation
- Over-exploitation of species
- Introduction or accidental release of exotic species that prove harmful to indigenous species
- Air and water pollution.

Over the coming decades human-induced climate change increasingly will become another major factor in reducing biological diversity. These pressures on biodiversity are, to a large extent, driven by economic development and related demands, including the increasing demand for biological resources.

Activities that reduce biodiversity jeopardize economic development and human health through losses of useful materials, genetic stocks, and the services of intact ecosystems. Material losses include food, wood, and medicines, as well as resources important for recreation and tourism. Genetic variation within species is the ultimate basis for evolution, the adaptation of wild populations to local environmental conditions, and the development of animal breeds and cultivated crop varieties which have yielded significant direct benefits to humanity.

Losing genetic diversity, like losing species diversity, makes it even more likely that further environmental disturbance will result in serious reductions in the goods and services that the Earth's ecosystems can provide. Decreased biodiversity also interferes with essential ecological services, such as pollination, maintenance of soil fertility, flood control, water purification, assimilation of wastes, and the cycling of carbon and other nutrients. Finally, in addition to the economic reasons for protecting biodiversity, many people feel a moral obligation

The government of Mexico is taking steps to protect an important migratory site of the Monarch butterfly.

17

not to destroy the other living organisms with which we share the Earth.

Deforestation and unsustainable use of forests

Forest ecosystems contain as much as 80 percent of the world's terrestrial biodiversity and provide wood fiber and biomass energy, as well as being critical components of the global cycles of water, energy, and nutrients. Forest ecosystems are being cleared and degraded at unsustainable rates in many parts of the world. One recent study estimates that only one-fifth of the world's original forests remain in an unmanaged state—most of these are found in Russia, Canada, and Brazil (see figure 9).

Over the past several centuries an estimated 60 percent of European forests, 30 percent of North American forests, and 35 percent of the former Soviet Union's forests have been cleared for long periods, primarily for agricultural purposes. While overall forest area in many mid-latitude temperate regions has increased over the past century (20 percent in the United States, 2 percent in Europe during 1971-1990, and about 1 percent globally during this period), the increase is in secondary growth and plantation forests.

The greatest rates of forest loss are now occurring in the species-rich tropics. More than one-fifth of the world's tropical forests have been cleared since 1960. Global rates of forest loss increased from about 12 million hectares per year in the 1970s to over 15 million hectares (0.8 percent of total natural forest cover) per year in the 1980s. During the 1990s, deforestation has been continuing at about 13 million hectares per year.

Current projections suggest that demand for wood will roughly double over the next 50 years, which will make increasing the use of sustainable forest practices more difficult. Even if such practices become more widespread, however, there is no guarantee that existing forests can sustainably increase their yield from the current production of 3 to 4 billion cubic meters of wood per year.

In addition to threats to biodiversity and potential shortages in the supply of forest products, the degradation of forests represents an enormous potential source of greenhouse gas emissions. Forest ecosystems contain about three times the amount of carbon currently present in the atmosphere— about one-third of this carbon is stored above ground (in trees and other vegetation), and two-thirds is stored in the soil. When forests are cleared or burned, much of this carbon is released into the atmosphere—according to current estimates, tropical deforestation and burning account for about one-quarter of carbon emissions into the atmosphere from human activities. Intensification of forest management in temperate and boreal forests has the

FIGURE 9

What happened to the forests that once covered the Earth?

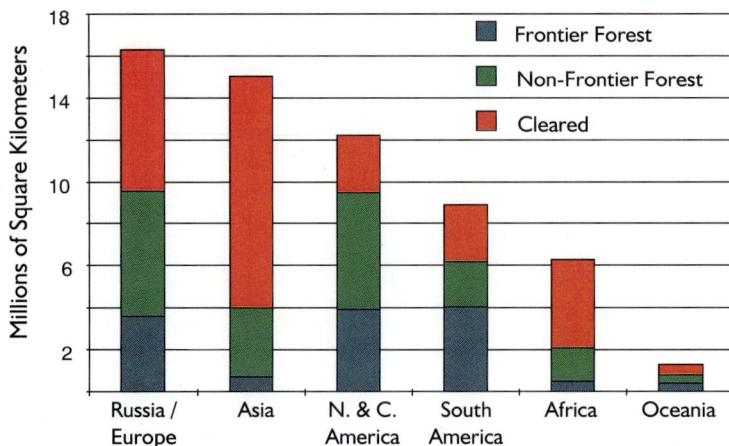

Source: D. Bryant, D. Nielsen, and L. Tangley. 1997. *The Last Frontier Forests.* World Resource Institute. Washington, DC.

potential to accelerate the release of carbon from the soil.

Desertification and land degradation

Roughly one-quarter of the Earth's terrestrial surface is used for crops, orchards, and rangelands. Over the past 40 to 50 years, land-cover and land-use changes (conversion of forests and grasslands to cropland, abandonment of agricultural lands) have been dramatic enough to be apparent from satellite images. Over the past few centuries land-use conversions, primarily changing grasslands and forests to agriculture, have contributed significant amounts of CO_2 to the atmosphere.

Another result of intensive use of land, particularly the world's arid and semi-arid lands, has been massive land degradation that has resulted in a marked decrease in soil fertility. This problem affects more than 900 million people in 100 countries, some of them among the least developed nations. Erosion, salinization, compaction, and other forms of degradation affect 30 percent of the world's irrigated lands, 40 percent of rainfed agricultural lands, and 70 percent of rangelands.

Desertification and land degradation result from poor land management, which can be exacerbated by climatic variations. Converting wild lands to agriculture often involves plowing the soils, which leads in temperate regions to an average decline in soil organic matter of between 25 and 40 percent over 25 years. Decreasing soil organic matter is almost always a clear indication of soil degradation, and often is accompanied by reductions in water infiltration, fertility, and ability to retain fertilizers. Plowing also exposes soils to wind and water erosion, resulting in large-scale pollution of freshwater resources. Tons of soil can be carried off of a single square kilometer of fertile land, contributing to degra-

Natural climatic variations can result in droughts that severely affect land productivity.

dation of freshwater lakes and rivers and eventually being carried into the sea. This soil loss reduces the intrinsic productivity of the land, forcing farmers to compensate by using higher fertilizer inputs to maintain crop yields.

Desertification and land degradation undermine the goal of sustainable development by increasing poverty, poor health, malnutrition, impaired child development, and susceptibility to disease. Severe desertification also can lead to large-scale migrations, which become sources of social tensions or cross-border security issues. The U.N. has estimated that over the next two decades 135 million people will face forced migration or famine as a result of food scarcity caused by soil infertility.

Freshwater degradation

About one-third of the world's population lives in countries that are experiencing moderate to high water stress, defined as when 20 to 40 percent of available freshwater is already being used. With

FIGURE 10
Water supply service coverage (percent of population served) at the end of 1994

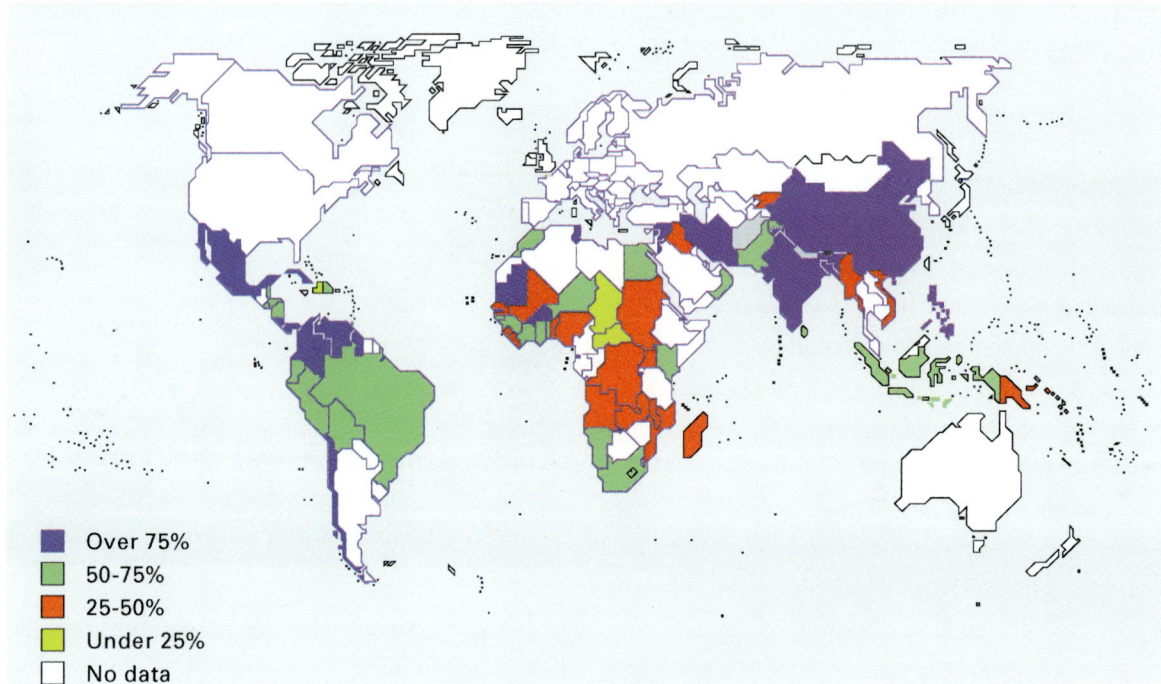

- Over 75%
- 50-75%
- 25-50%
- Under 25%
- No data

Note: The boundaries shown and the designations used on this map do not imply official endorsement or acceptance by the United Nations. The dotted line represents approximately the Line of Control in Jammu and Kashmir agreed upon by India and Pakistan. The final status of Jammu and Kashmir has not yet been agreed upon by the parties.
Source: WMO. 1997. *Comprehensive Assessment of the Freshwater Resources of the World.* Geneva.

increasing demands for water by a growing population, this fraction could rise to two-thirds of the world's population by the year 2025, with serious health implications. Currently, at least one-fifth of all people do not have access to safe drinking water, and about one-third lack adequate sanitation (see figure 10). At any given time an estimated one-half of the people in developing countries suffer from water- and food-related diseases caused either directly, by infection, or indirectly, by disease-carrying organisms that breed in water and food. The World Health Organization estimates that more than 5 million people die each year from diseases caused by unsafe drinking water and lack of water for sanitation and hygiene. These numbers include 3 million

young children who die from mostly water-borne diarrheal diseases.

Water shortages and water pollution cause widespread public health problems, limit economic and agricultural development, and harm a wide range of ecosystems. Maintaining sufficient supplies of fresh water for human uses (agriculture, household, and industrial uses) and natural ecosystems represents an increasing challenge for many societies. With large increases in both population and per capita use of water over the past century, efficient allocation of water resources among competing uses has become increasingly difficult. Some estimates show that by 2025, when the world population will likely have risen to more than 8 billion, almost all of the economically accessible water in the world may be required to meet the needs of agriculture, households, and industry, and to maintain ecosystem needs.

An important sector that is sensitive to the quantity and quality of freshwater supplies is irrigated agriculture. Seventy percent of the water withdrawn from lakes, rivers, and groundwater aquifers is already used for irrigation of agricultural lands, with much of this irrigation water used inefficiently due to evaporation or seepage. It is estimated that 80 percent of the additional food supplies required to feed the world's population over the next 30 years will depend on irrigation. Our ability to reduce freshwater degradation—through conservation, increased sewage and effluent treatment, reduced use of pesticides, cleaner industrial production, and application of demand management—will thus be key to meeting the global demand for food.

Marine environment and resource degradation

Oceans play a vital role in the global environment. Covering 70 percent of the Earth's surface, they influence global climate, food production, and

Marine fisheries are a major source of protein worldwide, but are under threat from over-exploitation.

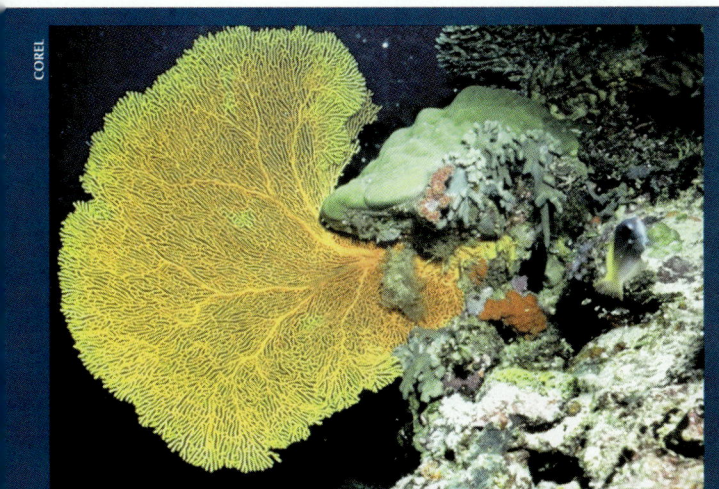

Coral reefs have been called the "rainforests of the sea" due to their biological richness.

economic activities worth trillions of dollars each year. Despite this vital role, coastal and marine systems are being rapidly degraded in many parts of the globe. In coastal areas, where human activities are concentrated, pollution, over-exploitation of resources, development of critical habitats such as wetlands and mangroves, and runoff from poor land-use practices have led to drastic reductions in nearshore fisheries production and aquatic biodiversity. Coastal marine environments also are showing signs of stress from increasing pollution from shipping and mining activities, agrochemical run-off, oil spills (600,000 tons/year), unsustainable fishing practices, and the introduction of alien species through ballast water. It is estimated that 10 percent of the world's coral reefs, which support about one third of the world's marine fish (93,000 species have been identified), already have been severely degraded; if current trends persist, one-third of the world's reefs will be destroyed within two decades. This decline in reef quality has serious biological impacts—including changes in the species composition and abundance of ecologically important marine animals and plants—with widespread social and economic implications for human populations that depend on these ecosystems.

Marine fishing contributes enormously to human survival by supplying more people with animal protein than any other source, but the resource is being over-used. The world fishing fleet has doubled since 1970, and 70 percent of the world's commercially important marine fish stocks are fully fished or overexploited. The wild marine fish catch peaked at 82 million tons in 1989, and since then has been slowly falling; this decline is leading to an increased reliance on aquaculture to meet the demand for fish for human consumption. In turn, increases in aquaculture are contributing to declining water quality in coastal areas and the loss of natural habitat, which is converted to fish and seafood farms. Maintaining present average per-capita consumption of seafood in the face of human population growth will require approximately 20 million additional tons of seafood annually by 2010.

Persistent organic pollutants

Persistent organic pollutants (POPs) are human-made compounds such as dioxins, DDT, PCBs, toxaphene, dieldrin, and hexachlorobenzene. They are used as pesticides and in industrial processes, or are generated as by-products of combustion. Their chemical structure allows them to persist in the environment, resisting natural degradation. They can be carried long distances by winds and water currents and in migrating animals, and can build up in the tissues of living organisms to harmful levels.

POPs accumulate in the fatty tissues of a wide range of organisms, particularly predators at the top of the food chain. Some of these compounds have been shown to cause cancers and birth defects, increase infertility, and interfere with endocrine, hormonal, and immune system functioning. Well-documented examples of the damage to wildlife

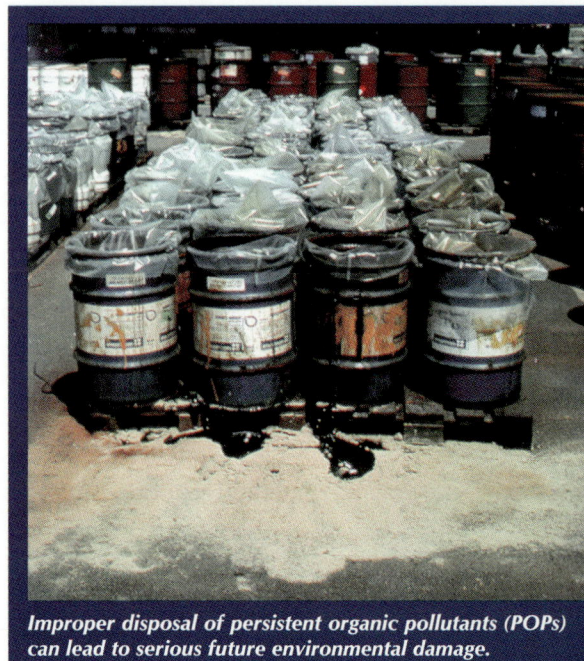

Improper disposal of persistent organic pollutants (POPs) can lead to serious future environmental damage.

caused by POPs include declines in bird populations due to eggshell thinning, poisoning of many aquatic and terrestrial organisms, and the accumulation of pesticides in the fatty tissues of marine mammals. People exposed to high levels of these toxic chemicals also have suffered a wide range of health effects. Most at risk are humans who eat food contaminated by the chemicals.

The Rotterdam Convention on the Prior Informed Consent Procedure for Certain Hazardous Chemicals and Pesticides in International Trade was signed in 1998, and there are ongoing talks sponsored by United Nations Environment Program (UNEP) on establishing an international POPs treaty; a second round of negotiations is scheduled to be held in February 1999. A number of governments have banned the use of these organic compounds because of their toxicity and environmental persistence. However, some POPs, such as DDT and PCBs, are still widely used in parts of the world, and stockpiles of old chemicals have been left to seep into the environment. Even when the sources of chemicals are eliminated, these compounds can cycle through living organisms for decades.

LINKAGES AMONG THE ENVIRONMENTAL ISSUES

Human societies have traditionally addressed each environmental issue in isolation. A better understanding of the linkages among these different issues is necessary if we are to avoid making decisions that simply benefit one environmental issue at the

FIGURE 11

Linkages among environmental issues

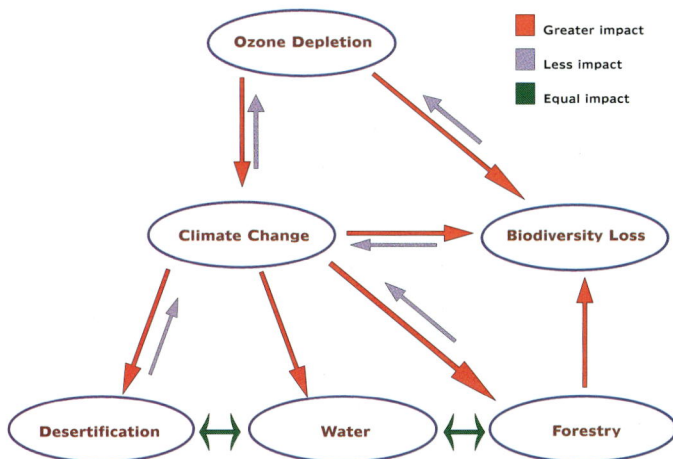

expense of others (see figure 11). The following section illustrates current scientific understanding of the linkages among global issues (see box D).

Climate change, loss of biological diversity, and forestry

There are a number of feedback loops in the interactions among climate, biodiversity, and forests. For example, changes in climate affect the boundaries, composition, and functioning of ecological systems,

---

Box D

International scientific assessments

The scientific bases for these linkages have been drawn from international scientific assessments that have been conducted over the past 10 years, involving thousands of experts from academia, governments, U.N. agencies, industry, and environmental nongovernment organizations. Some key international scientific assessments include the following:

- UNEP/WMO Intergovernmental Panel on Climate Change: 1990, 1992, 1995, 1997, 1998 (third assessment report to be completed in 2001)
- UNEP/WMO Stratospheric Ozone Depletion: 1981, 1985, 1988, 1989, 1991, 1992, 1994, and 1998
- UNEP Global Biodiversity Assessment: 1995
- UNEP/WMO: Interactions of Desertification and Climate, 1996
- UN/SEI: Comprehensive Freshwater Assessment, 1997
- FAO/UNEP: Forests Resources Assessment (1990; second assessment under preparation)
- FAO: State of World Fisheries and Aquaculture, 1996
- Group of Experts on Scientific Aspects of Marine Pollution (GESAMP) Assessment on Land-Based Activities and Their Impacts on the Marine Environment (to be completed in 1999)
- GESAMP State of the Marine Environment Assessment (to be completed in 2000)
- UNEP Global International Water Assessment (to be completed in 2002)
- POPs Assessment (under preparation).

These international assessments, in turn, have been based on the advances in understanding that have resulted from the planning and implementation of a large number of national and international programs of scientific research over the last 25 years. These include the World Climate Research Program, the International Geosphere-Biosphere Programme, and Diversitas.

---

including forests; and changes in the structure and functioning of forests affect the Earth's climate system through changes in biogeochemical cycles, particularly cycles of carbon and nitrogen.

How changes in climate affect biological diversity, forests, and aquatic ecosystems

Climate, biological diversity, and forests have always been inextricably linked. As climate warms, species will migrate toward higher latitudes and altitudes in both hemispheres, and the species composition and functioning of the ecosystems will change in response to changing climatic conditions and increases in the abundance of carbon dioxide. The amount of carbon dioxide in the air affects the physiological functioning of plants, particularly the efficiency with which they use water. Recently developed computer models of ecosystem behavior under changed climate conditions and increased carbon dioxide show large changes in the distribution, composition, and abundance of major biomes (see figure 13).

If the climate changes rapidly, as projected, mismatches may occur between the new climatic conditions and plants that have adapted to current conditions over the course of centuries. Even in areas where the type of ecosystem does not change—a forest remains a forest—there may be large changes in species distribution and losses in biological diversity at the species level (see figure 12). The Intergovernmental Panel on Climate Change projected that with a sustained increase in mean surface temperature of only 2 to 3 degrees Centigrade—which is a smaller increase than many climate models predict with doubled carbon dioxide levels—there would be changes in species composition in about one-third of the current forest areas of the world. These changes would affect one-seventh of the current tropical forest and two-thirds of current boreal forested areas.

Questions exist about how quickly forest species will be able to adapt to the projected rapid changes in climatic conditions. Ecological models suggest that the boundaries of ecological systems could move poleward by 150 to 650 kilometers during the next century; this is more rapid than the

FIGURE 12

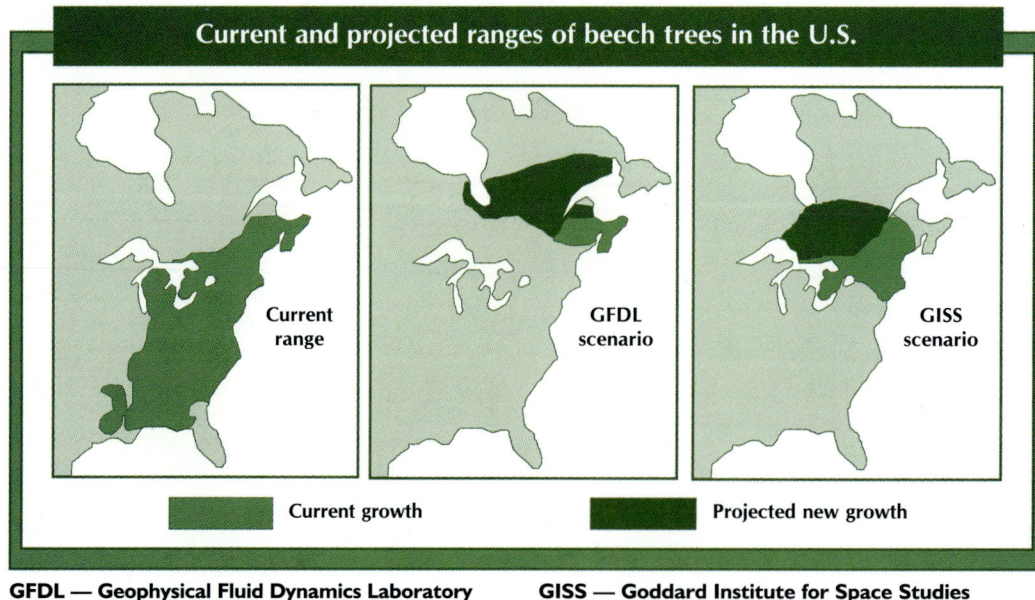

Current and projected ranges of beech trees in the U.S.

Current range

GFDL scenario

GISS scenario

Current growth

Projected new growth

GFDL — Geophysical Fluid Dynamics Laboratory   **GISS — Goddard Institute for Space Studies**

Source: U.S. Environmental Protection Agency.

FIGURE 13

Changes in ecosystems

MAPSS — Major world biomes, current climate

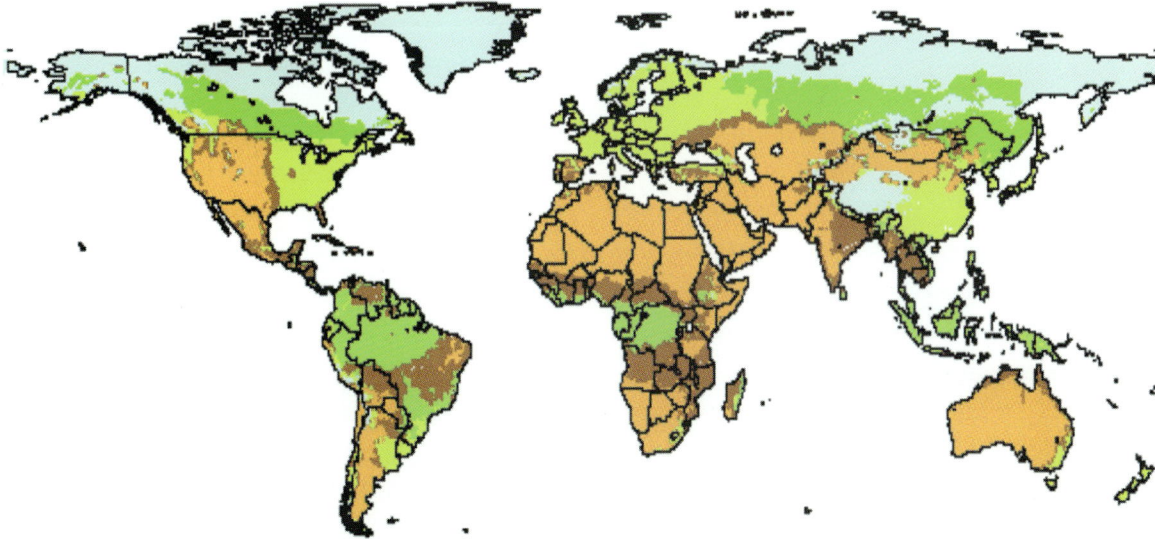

MAPSS — Major world biomes, GFDL future climate scenario

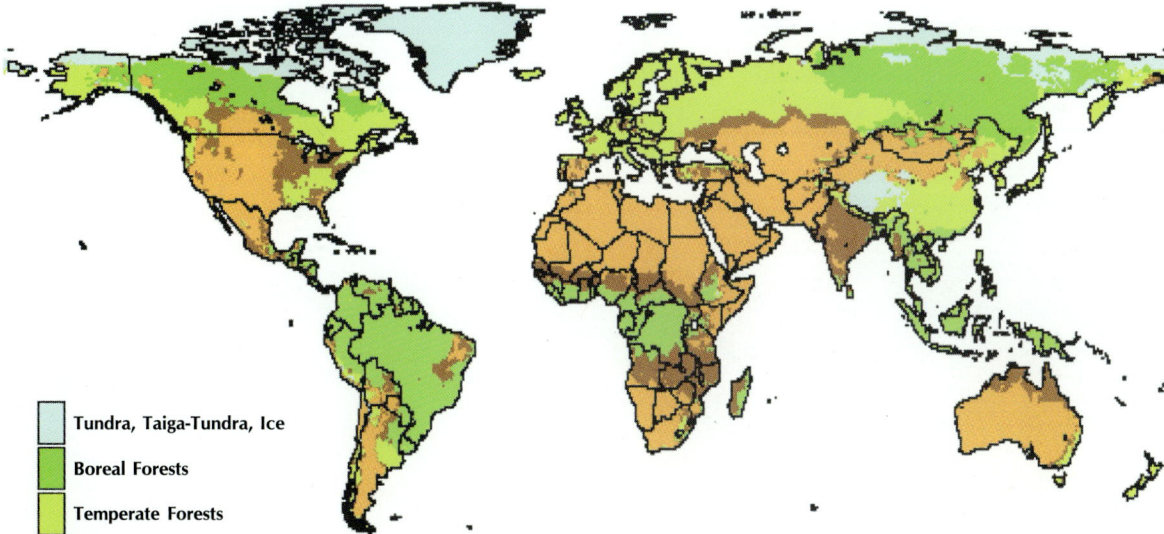

Tundra, Taiga-Tundra, Ice

Boreal Forests

Temperate Forests

Tropical Forests

Savannas, Dry Forests, Woodlands

Grasslands, Shrublands, Deserts

Source: Adapted from: Neilson, R.P. and D. Marks, 1994: A global perspective of regional vegetation and hydrologic sensitivities from climatic change. Journal of Vegetation Science, 5, 715-730.

migration rates of 4 to 200 kilometers per century achieved by tree species after the retreat of the last ice age. Although migration rates may be sufficient to keep up with projected climate changes in areas of continuous forests, it is unlikely that many species will be able to migrate through the sparse and fragmented forest patches that are now typical in so many parts of the world. There is a concern that temporary diebacks may occur in a number of species prior to re-establishment, accompanied by large releases of carbon dioxide that would further accelerate the rate of climate change. The diebacks would have a wide array of ecological and economic impacts.

Aquatic ecosystems, particularly coral reefs, mangrove swamps, and coastal wetlands are vulnerable to changes in climate (see figure 14). In principle, coral reefs—the most biologically diverse marine systems—are potentially vulnerable to changes in both sea level and ocean temperature. While most coral systems should be able to grow at a sufficient pace to survive a 15 to 95 centimeter sea-level rise over the next century, a sustained increase of several degrees Centigrade would threaten the long-term viability of many of these systems.

How changes in land use and forests affect climate

Replacing a forest with agricultural fields changes the energy and water balance of the landscape, generally resulting in higher surface temperatures due to reductions in evapotranspiration. Local and regional climate can be affected quite strongly, as less water is released into the air through evapotranspiration to form clouds that can produce rain.

These local changes also can have regional and global effects. The conversion from forest to crops results in a net release of carbon to the atmosphere due to a decrease in aboveground living biomass, as well as the oxidation of organic matter in the soils as they are cultivated and exposed to the air. This carbon increases the overall atmospheric concentration of greenhouse gases, thereby exacerbating the greenhouse effect. The contribution of land-use changes to global emissions of greenhouse gases varies with changing patterns of land-use. Currently, emissions of carbon dioxide from deforestation and other land-use changes contribute about 25 percent of total global carbon dioxide emissions from human activities.

Global greenhouse gas emissions could also be affected by climate-induced changes in the structure and functioning of ecological systems, resulting in large amounts of carbon being released to the atmosphere. Fluxes of methane and nitrous oxide, two potent greenhouse gases, may also increase from these climate-induced changes in ecological systems, further accelerating climate change. As a result of increasing temperatures, melting permafrost could lead to very large releases of carbon to

---

FIGURE 14

Loss of coastal wetlands

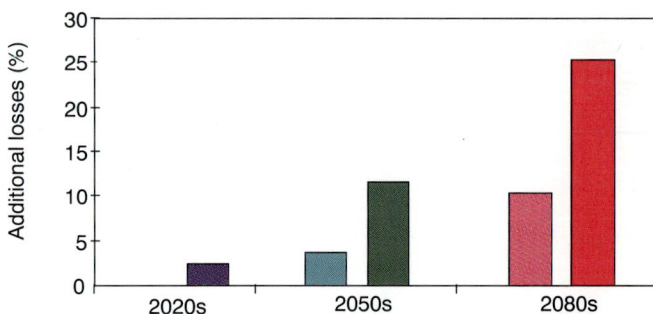

Percentage additional losses of coastal wetlands due to the sea-level rise scenario assuming low-loss (left bar) and high-loss (right bar) scenarios.

Source: R. Nicholls, Middlesex University in the U.K. Meteorological Office. 1997. *Climate Change and Its Impacts: A Global Perspective.* Brittanic Crown Copyright.

the atmosphere in the form of methane and carbon dioxide. In addition, reductions in forest cover would increase local albedo and decrease rates of evaporation and evapotranspiration, with a tendency to make the local and regional climates hotter and drier.

Currently, emissions of carbon dioxide resulting from land-use changes in the tropics are approximately balanced by an increased uptake of carbon by the large areas of regrowing forests in the Northern Hemisphere. Higher atmospheric carbon dioxide concentrations and deposition of atmospheric nitrogen may even enhance the growth of these forests. Yet continued clearing of the world's forests would reduce the global sink from forest growth, further increasing the rate of climate change.

Climate change and water resources

One of the most important impacts of climate change is alteration of the global hydrological cycle, upon which we depend for freshwater supplies. There is no doubt that in a warmer world there will be an intensification of the hydrological cycle, with an increase in precipitation and evapotranspiration on a global scale and changes in patterns of where and when precipitation falls (see figure 15). Unfortunately, current climate models cannot provide an accurate picture of how water resources will change at the local level. Most models suggest that there will be an increase in winter precipitation, an increase in the amount of water falling in heavy precipitation events (more than 5 centimeters in 24

FIGURE 15

Observed change in annual precipitation for the 2050s

The change in annual precipitation for the 2050s compared with the present day, when the climate model is driven with an increase in greenhouse gas concentrations equivalent to about 1% increase per year in CO_2. This illustration shows the average of four model runs with different starting conditions.

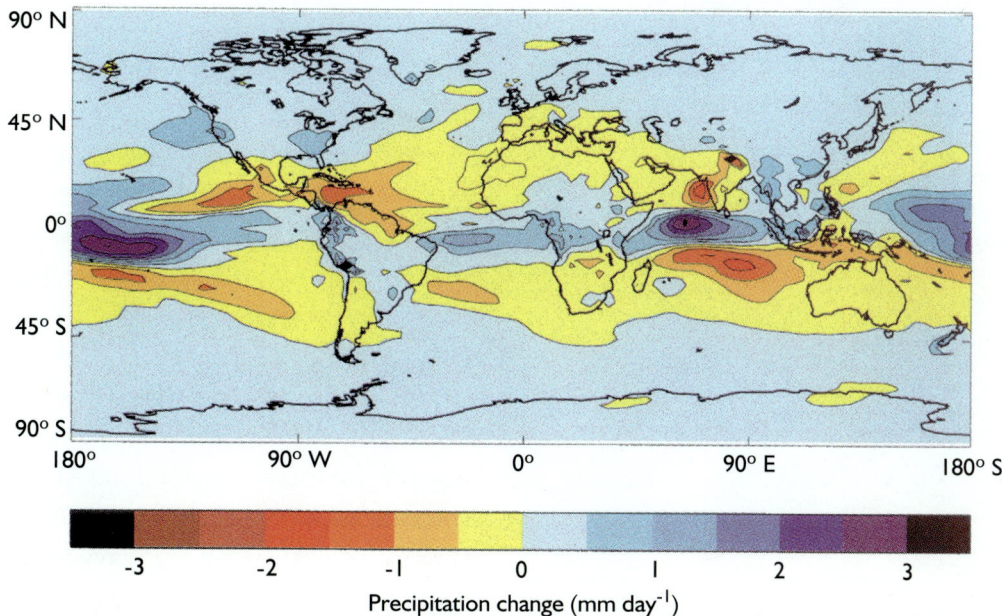

Precipitation change (mm day^{-1})

Source: R. Nicholls, Middlesex University in the U.K. Meteorological Office. 1997. *Climate Change and Its Impacts: A Global Perspective.* Brittanic Crown Copyright.

hours), and an increase in evaporation and evapo-transpiration. Hence, in many regions increases in both floods and droughts are likely, and many areas that are arid and semi-arid today will be even drier in the future—all of which could decrease available water supply (see figure 16).

FIGURE 16
Change in water stress

Change in water stress, due to climate change, in countries using more than 20% of their potential water resources.

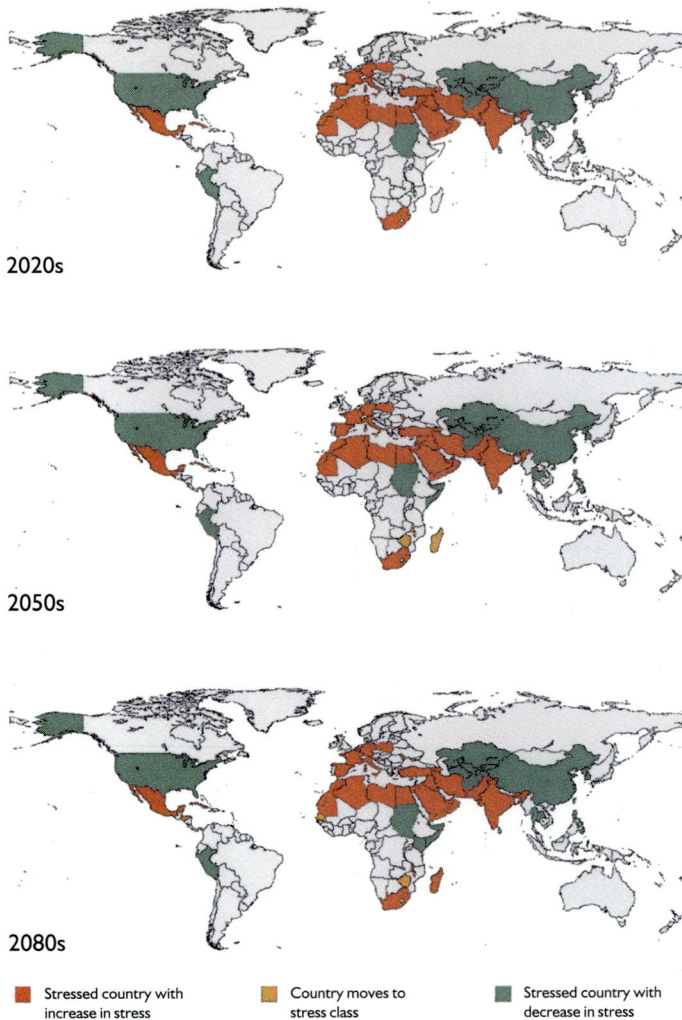

2020s

2050s

2080s

| ■ Stressed country with increase in stress | ■ Country moves to stress class | ■ Stressed country with decrease in stress |

Source: N. Arnell and R. King, University of Southampton in the U.K. Meteorological Office. 1997. *Climate Change and Its Impacts: A Global Perspective.* Brittanic Crown Copyright.

Biodiversity, forest loss, and water resources

Losses of biodiversity can take many forms, one of which is the large-scale loss of habitat that results from conversion of forests to agricultural lands. This change from trees to crops affects many biophysical and biogeochemical processes. For example, cultivated soils generally have a lower water-holding capacity than the forests that preceded them. Such a reduction in water-holding capacity results in more flooding, as water moves off the fields and into rivers and streams at a much faster rate. Increased flooding leads to a greater need for managing the flow of rivers, including dam building, to avoid flood damage and maintain water supply in periods of reduced flow. The conversion of forests to fields also usually results in greater loss of topsoil through erosion, partly because of the change from perennial trees to annual crops. The topsoil also is more vulnerable to erosion due to an associated decrease in organic matter and the number of roots capable of holding the soil, as well as the physical effects of plowing. The eroded soil can quickly enter waterways, leading to further degradation of water resources as a result of forest conversion. The loss of deep-rooted trees also reduces the amount of water that is able to infiltrate to deeper soil layers.

Loss of forest biodiversity can result from habitat loss, fragmentation, and over-harvesting of plant and animal species. These losses of particular species in forests may not have the immediate or dramatic effects that large-scale conversion to other uses may have. However, the loss of species richness can increase the vulnerability of forest ecosystems to other environmental stresses, such as disease, pollution, wind, and flooding. If keystone species are lost, dramatic reorganizations of entire forest ecosystems can occur, changing the ecosystem services on which humans depend.

While the risks of adverse changes to forests are high, given current trends, some forest management strategies could stop the release of carbon, and even increase its capture, by increasing forest growth. Such sustainability strategies have the added benefit of preserving habitat, thus favoring the maintenance of biodiversity and increasing the ability of the landscape to retain water, consequently protecting against flooding and moderating the local climate. Managing forest ecosystems wisely can thus yield multiple environmental gains.

Desertification and its links to other global issues

Climate change and higher rates of land degradation/desertification can exacerbate each other through positive feedbacks. These interactions are likely to have strong negative impacts on land productivity, food supply, biodiversity, and fresh-water availability, particularly in dry regions.

Desertification and land degradation can contribute to local warming by reducing plant cover and increasing soil exposure, which changes the energy balance of an area. Given the large area of degraded drylands, the net impact of these local shifts in energy balance can be felt on a regional to global scale.

Deserts, semi-arid lands, and dry woodlands also constitute a large potential source of carbon emissions into the atmosphere. The drylands of the world store 240 billion tons of organic carbon in their soils and vegetation—40 times the amount of carbon released by humans from fossil deposits every year. Vigorous efforts to control desertification would not only ensure that existing carbon in these ecosystems is maintained, but could lead to net annual carbon sequestration. Such a shift in the carbon storage of dryland areas would not only help to reduce the rate of climate change, but also would increase agricultural productivity in these areas.

Changes in climate, in turn, can intensify desertification and land degradation. These processes are exacerbated by variations in weather, and climate change can increase such variability. If climate change continues unabated, the potential increase in the frequency and intensity of droughts would reinforce the vulnerability of dryland ecosystems, increasing rates of desertification and further threatening the security of food and fiber supplies in many regions. If more vegetation were removed from these dryland areas, available soil moisture would also be reduced. Runoff would occur more frequently and the soil would dry out more quickly. Decreases in vegetation cover also would lead to increased soil erosion, reducing agricultural production while increasing siltation rates of reservoirs and decreasing freshwater availability.

Finally, the biodiversity of dryland areas is directly threatened by desertification and land degradation. As agricultural productivity decreases on existing farms, there is increased pressure to convert more natural ecosystems to agricultural uses, and thus destroy the habitat of animals and plants. If rates of desertification accelerate because of climate change, the loss of biodiversity in these regions will also accelerate. This is a critical concern for food supplies, as almost all of the globally important cereal grains originate from drylands. The loss of the genetic forebears of these critical food plants could impair our ability to adapt their genome to accommodate a changing environment.

Stratospheric ozone depletion, climate change, and biodiversity

Stratospheric ozone depletion and climate change are connected in three primary ways. First, many of the same gases affect the ozone layer and contribute to the greenhouse effect. Some of the gases that chemically affect stratospheric ozone—chlorofluorocarbons (CFCs), methane, and nitrous oxide—are more powerful greenhouse gases, on a per-molecule basis, than is carbon dioxide. CFCs and nitrous oxide are of particular concern in terms of their effect on the radiative balance of the atmosphere, due to their long lifetimes. In addition, greenhouse gases cool the stratosphere and enhance the chemical destruction of ozone by chlorinated and brominated chemicals, thus extending the expected time needed for the recovery of the stratospheric ozone layer by a decade or more.

Second, reductions in ozone concentrations in the lower stratosphere cool the atmosphere at those altitudes, and partly offset the warming in the lower troposphere. Third, depletion of stratospheric ozone leads to an increase in the level of ultraviolet-B (UV-B) radiation reaching the Earth's surface, which can affect terrestrial and aquatic biogeochemical cycles—thus altering both sources and sinks of greenhouse gases and chemically important trace gases. These potential changes to atmosphere-biosphere interactions could either mitigate or reinforce the atmospheric build-up of these gases.

Stratospheric ozone depletion affects terrestrial and aquatic ecosystems through its influence on surface ultraviolet radiation. UV-B radiation directly and indirectly affects the physiological and developmental processes of plants, thus influencing plant growth, plant form, and the biomass allocation within plants. The response of plants to UV-B varies considerably among species and among cultivars of the same species. In agricultural systems, an increase in UV-B radiation will necessitate using cultivars more tolerant to UV-B; in grasslands and forests, such an increase will likely result in changes in species composition, with implications for biodiversity. Ecosystem-level effects, such as changes in competitive balance, herbivory, plant pathogens, and biogeochemical cycles, also are expected. Increased levels of UV-B radiation reduce the production of marine phytoplankton, which are predominantly found in high latitudes and upwelling areas on the continental shelves. Phytoplankton is the foundation of aquatic food webs and a major sink for atmospheric carbon dioxide. UV-B radiation also has been found to cause damage to fish, shrimp, crabs, amphibians, and other marine animals during their early developmental stages.

Part III

MEETING HUMAN NEEDS WITHIN THE ENVIRONMENTAL ENVELOPE

HUMAN APPROPRIATION AND manipulation of the Earth's resources produce the materials and services that we always have depended on to fulfill our basic needs and our aspirations for a better quality of life. The simple act of fulfilling these human needs always has had some environmental impacts. In some cases, those impacts have grown to the point that they are undermining our environmental life support system.

This environmental degradation poses a dual set of challenges: reducing current human impacts on the environment while ensuring that people have equitable access to resources to meet their needs. Meeting these challenges will mean that the very poor get a fair share of the world's ecological goods and services.

People need adequate food, clean water and energy, sanitation, safe shelter, education, and satisfying work. In addition to meeting today's needs, we are faced with preparing for a global population that is growing at the rate of about 80 million people per year, and is expected to increase by 50 to 70 percent by the middle of the next century.

This section of the report explores how efforts to meet a series of basic human needs influence the global environment, often causing or accelerating degradation at scales from local to global. It also examines how global environmental problems create feedbacks that undercut the measures employed to meet human needs. Finally, for each of the sectors explored, the section reviews the potential for "win-win" strategies that could simultaneously help to meet basic human needs and protect the environment.

MEETING THE DEMAND FOR FOOD

The demand for food is a pressing concern in the face of global population growth.

As the human population grows and standards of living increase, the need for food will continue to grow along with them.

Effects of agricultural production on the global environment

Past strategies for increasing agricultural production have included converting wildlands to croplands (extensification), using chemical fertilizers to increase yields (intensification), and using irrigation to increase yields or enable cultivation of otherwise non-arable land. Increasing food production in the future will require some combination of these strategies, each of which have risks that will need to be minimized by careful management (see figure 17).

Expanding the land under cultivation results in a loss of biodiversity, as diverse ecosystems are converted to fields growing only a few species (usually exotics). When forest systems are converted to agricultural uses, a net loss of carbon to the atmosphere accompanies the deforestation, as trees are replaced by grasses or crops. This clearing also increases flooding, as the new agricultural systems retain less precipitation than did the forests. Extending cultivation into natural habitats can lead to the fragmentation of remaining intact habitats; proliferation of invasive, weedy species; and degradation of soils.

Intensification of crop production can involve a variety of chemical treatments, the most common of which are nitrogen fertilizers, both synthetic and natural. The side effects of applying these fertilizers include the release of nitrogen gases (some of which are strong greenhouse gases) to the atmosphere and nitrogen runoff into watersheds. Nitrogen runoff is considered carcinogenic at high levels and can cause eutrophication, depleting oxygen in freshwater ecosystems.

Irrigation is another strategy for increasing agricultural production. Expanding irrigation systems, however, increases the demand for fresh water, in some cases leading to shortages and conflict over water-use rights. If poorly managed, especially on thin soils in semi-arid or arid climates, extensive irrigation can lead to land degradation and salinization of soils. Any strategy for meeting the need for in-

FIGURE 17

Linkages among food production and global environmental issues

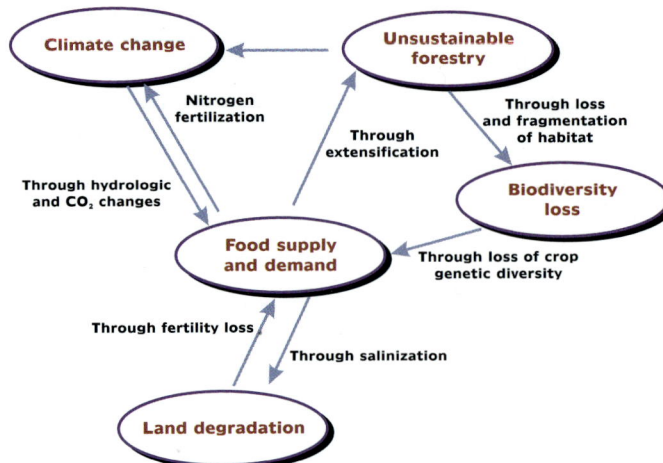

creased agricultural production has the potential to increase global rates of biodiversity loss, climate change, and desertification.

Effects of global environmental issues on food production

Global environmental changes will have a number of impacts on agricultural productivity, which is already limited by climatic factors such as water availability (such as quantity and timing of rainfall relative to crop development) and the length of the growing season. The most recent IPCC assessment concluded that, while climate-induced changes in global agricultural productivity are unlikely to be large in comparison with overall production (due in part to the availability of adaptation options, see figure 18), changes in the climate system and atmospheric CO_2 concentrations may have relatively large regional effects on agricultural productivity. Changes in temperature and precipitation patterns may restrict agriculture in some areas and benefit others; and a large body of research demonstrates that higher atmospheric concentrations of CO_2 can

enhance crop productivity, if nutrients and water are in adequate supply. These physical and physiological influences may interact in the future to identify which regions are suited for intensive agriculture, resulting in generally poleward shifts of agricultural productivity in the mid-latitudes. These changes could have strong adverse effects on the capacity of many regions and even some nations to feed themselves. There may be increased risk of hunger and famine in some locations—particularly in subtropical and tropical areas dependent on isolated agricultural systems such as sub-Saharan Africa; south, east, and southeast Asia; tropical areas of Latin America; and some Pacific island nations (see figure 19).

Agriculture faces another threat stemming from the need to feed a growing human population: a loss of genetic diversity among agricultural crops, with potentially negative effects on agricultural sustainability. Intensive agriculture relies on heavy applications of fertilizers and pesticides to large areas of genetically similar monocultures. However, these monocultures are susceptible to outbreaks of

FIGURE 18

Effects on agricultural productivity with different levels of adaptation

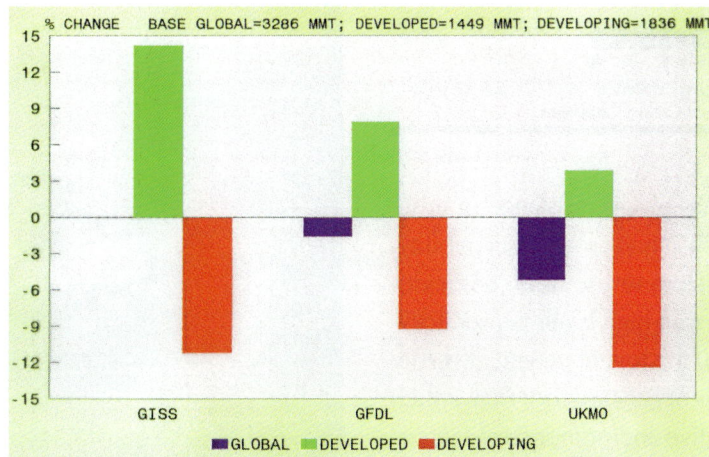

Source: C. Rosezweig and M. Parry. 1994. "Potential Impacts of Climate Change on World Food Supply." *Nature,* 367:133–138.

ing technologies in the industrialized world—such as precision agriculture, in which satellite and GIS technologies are used by farmers to target applications of chemicals—can result in greatly increased efficiency in the use of agricultural fertilizers and pesticides, thus enabling yields to be maintained or enhanced without increasing the overall use of chemical additives. These advanced technologies result in reduced greenhouse gas emissions, and at the same time maintain or increase agricultural production. In many parts of the world these high-tech solutions are not appropriate, and other traditional approaches are more likely to succeed. In several developing countries, governments and community development organizations are joining forces to implement strategies for promoting rural development and sustainable agriculture that also have benefits for biodiversity, climate, water resources, and forest conservation. These strategies include support for sustainable intensification and communal production activities; establishment of projects to conserve forests, fisheries, and protected areas; and development of a coherent land-use framework that integrates these objectives and builds community support.

On a global basis, the use of sustainable agricultural strategies could result in cleaner agriculture, with associated benefits to water quality, biodiversity, health, and human welfare. The potential crediting of increases in carbon sequestration in agricultural and pasture lands under Article 3.4 of the Kyoto Protocol could provide additional incentives for farmers to move toward more sustainable techniques, resulting in economic benefits as well as environmental gains by reducing the threat of climate disruption, biodiversity loss, and increased desertification.

MEETING DEMANDS FOR FIBER AND WOOD

Demands for fiber and wood products are growing steadily, fueled by a growing population and demands for a better quality of life. In the future, increased use of wood and fiber in energy production—as an alternative to fossil fuels—will likely combine with population and economic growth to further increase the rate of growth in demand.

Effects of fiber and wood production on global environmental issues

Meeting human demand for fiber and wood products results in a net release of carbon dioxide to the atmosphere, which contributes to climate change. Harvesting forests results in the replacement of mature forests by smaller, younger trees or by other types of vegetation—both of which contain much less carbon. It also results in a loss of habitat as well as fragmentation of remaining habitat, resulting in declines in biodiversity. Activities undertaken to

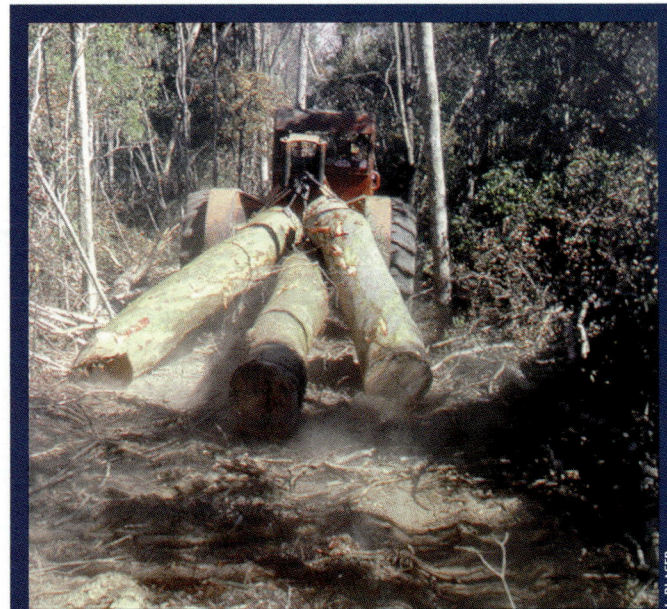

Timber harvesting can have important effects on both the forest and hydrologic systems.

meet wood and fiber needs also can affect local environmental conditions. For example, they may accelerate erosion and topsoil loss by removing physically stabilizing root systems and energy-absorbing forest canopies, and by reducing the capacity of the soils of these systems to absorb rainwater, and hence control the intensity with which it runs off, into, and over soil. Increased runoff carries large amounts of soil into nearby waterways, decreasing the fertility of the originally forested landscape and making forest regeneration more difficult.

The overall release of carbon, loss of habitat and biodiversity, and effects on soil structure and fertility from forest harvest depend on the forest-management strategies employed. As with increasing agricultural production, yields from forests can be improved by either expanding the area harvested or increasing the harvest intensity within existing stands. In the case of commercial forestry, management choices can help minimize environmental impacts. Intensifying management of forests that are already intensively harvested for timber and pulp will have less severe impacts than converting new areas of natural forest to industrial forestry. However, much of the world's harvest of forest products is carried out by small landowners and local residents, who harvest wood for domestic uses, such as fuel. The amount of wood harvested for these uses is increasing globally, often resulting in the loss or serious degradation of local forest resources, with attendant environmental effects.

Effects of global environmental issues on fiber and wood production

Climate change and biodiversity losses, in turn, affect the production of fiber and wood. Both changes in temperature and rainfall and increases in atmospheric concentrations of CO_2 can affect forest growth and productivity. Computer simulations suggest that, at least in Northern Hemisphere temperate and boreal latitudes, the climate zones for temperate deciduous and boreal forests generally will move poleward. Current temperate deciduous forests may become more savanna-like—drier and grassier—as overall water availability decreases.

Loss of biodiversity as a result of more intensive management is likely to make forest ecosystems more susceptible to stresses associated with other environmental problems. While plant growth may not change significantly, ecosystem performance—including the ability to resist or recover from diseases and pests—will be affected by reductions in biological diversity. Therefore, even in the absence of climatic change, loss of diversity is likely to weaken the resilience of forests, reducing their long-term capacity for wood and fiber production.

Opportunities for multiple benefits

Opportunities for more sustainable management of forest resources are similar to those for agriculture. One broad strategy is to recognize and exploit the multiple uses and services—including timber supply, wildlife habitat, recreational resources, and watershed management—provided by forested land. Adaptive management strategies that seek to maximize a sustainable stream of revenues from multiple uses of the same landscape can have a lower overall environmental impact than intensive harvesting alone. These include strategies that increase the realization of economic value to local communities from sustainable harvesting of non-timber products (such as edible and medicinal plants, or resins) from forests. Another approach to recognizing the multiple uses and values of forest resources is to create markets for the ecological goods and services they provide. For example, opportunities for trading greenhouse gas emissions reductions through joint implementation and possibly the Clean Development Mechanism envisioned in the Kyoto Protocol to the U.N. Framework Convention on Climate Change have the potential to create markets for carbon sequestered in forested lands.

Efficient carbon management in forest ecosystems can have multiple environmental benefits (such as mitigation of the greenhouse effect and improved watershed management), as well as economic benefits (improved productivity). Carbon is stored in both trees and forest soils. As reported by the IPCC in its Second Assessment Report, the greatest potential for sequestering large amounts of carbon is in tropical and sub-tropical countries, but this potential depends critically on slowing tropical deforestation in the near term.

Since demand for wood will continue to rise as population grows, gains in efficiency of harvesting and forest management practices also could be important. There is potential for efficiency improvements in the harvesting process that could decrease the number of trees that have to be cut to produce the same amount of timber. Establishment of efficient plantations on already deforested lands could also help to take the pressure off remaining primary forests, particularly if carried out in the context of a landscape approach to forest management.

MEETING DEMANDS FOR WATER

Fresh water is essential for human health, food production, and sanitation, as well as for manufacturing and other industrial uses. At least one-fifth of all people do not have access to safe drinking water, and more than one-half—particularly those living in poverty—lack adequate sanitation. As a result, about one-half of the people living in developing countries suffer from water- and food-related diseases.

Water is also one of the basic needs for the survival of terrestrial and aquatic ecosystems.

The number of regions in the world where human demands exceed local water supplies is growing. According to the 1997 U.N. Comprehensive Freshwater Assessment, global water use has been growing at more than twice the rate of the population increase during this century; already a number of regions are experiencing chronic water shortages. There are currently more than 430 million people living in countries considered "water stressed," i.e., where availability of fresh water per person per year sinks below approximately 1,700 cubic meters, leading to chronic and widespread water shortages. According to some estimates (based on UN 1996 medium population projections), the percentage of the world's population in countries experiencing water stress could increase more than

FIGURE 20

World population in freshwater scarcity, stress, and relative sufficiency in 1995 and 2050

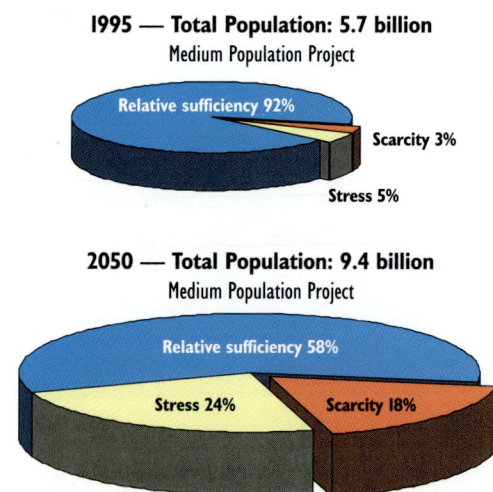

1995 — Total Population: 5.7 billion
Medium Population Project

Relative sufficiency 92%
Scarcity 3%
Stress 5%

2050 — Total Population: 9.4 billion
Medium Population Project

Relative sufficiency 58%
Stress 24%
Scarcity 18%

Note: Pie size is proportional to the world population in the designated year.
Source: T. Gardner-Outlaw and R. Engelman, 1997. *Sustaining Water, Easing Scarcity: A Second Update.* Population Action International. Washington, DC.

fivefold, from about 8 percent in 1995 to some 40 percent in 2050 (see figure 20). Water scarcity could be one of the major factors limiting our ability to increase food production to feed the growing population.

Effects of meeting water needs on environmental issues

Using water resources in an unsustainable manner can hamper economic productivity and social development in a region. Extracting water from underground sources faster than nature can replenish it has caused aquifers in many regions to recede deeper underground, making continued access to the water increasingly difficult and expensive. This can force people to use lower-quality water sources and reduce the underground flow of water into rivers. Reduction of available surface or underground water (groundwater) can lead to land degradation and desertification. Groundwater depletion also can cause land subsidence and, in coastal areas, lead to saltwater intrusion and contamination of freshwater aquifers. Water withdrawals from rivers and streams can lead to reduced flow and periodic drying, with potentially negative effects on aquatic biodiversity.

Effects of global environmental issues on water

Changes in climate are likely to make freshwater management even more difficult. Climate change is expected to alter the overall amount, frequency, and variability of precipitation around the world. Even though climate warming will inevitably "speed up" the hydrologic cycle, increasing rates of evaporation and amounts of precipitation on a global scale, the regional distribution of this precipitation may change, leaving some areas much wetter, and others much drier. While projections of the regional and local effects of climate change on water re-

sources are uncertain at present, all global climate models show a tendency to mid-continental warming and drying, resulting from increased temperatures and evapotranspiration. Some calculations suggest that reductions in available soil moisture may be equivalent to major agricultural droughts (see figure 21).

FIGURE 21
Percent reduction in June-August soil moisture

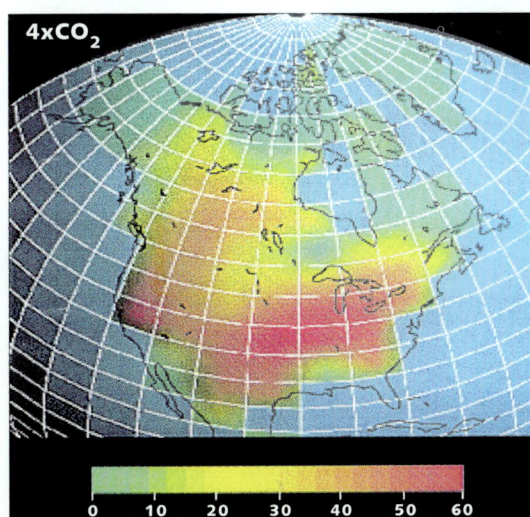

Source: Office of Science and Technology Policy. Washington, D.C.

For regions whose water supplies depend on dams, both the timing and form of precipitation are important. In regions that currently depend on mountain snowpack to store water and then release it during snowmelt into dammed watersheds, a switch from snow to winter rain could make it harder to store sufficient water in the spring to avoid late summer drought. If the variability or severity of storms increases, as exhibited in some models, many regions may lack the infrastructure to manage the supply of water and prevent flooding.

Conversion of natural ecosystems to less diverse agricultural systems or to suburban or urban

Irrigation helps farmers to increase production when rainfall is insufficient or uncertain.

environments reduces the land's ability to absorb and hold precipitation. Converted areas are often more prone to floods during rainy periods, because of increased rates of runoff, and to water scarcity during periods of low precipitation.

One of the undervalued services provided by natural landscapes, particularly wetlands, is the filtration of wastes from and detoxification of runoff before it reaches waterways. Due to this important ability to purify water, as well as the critical role played by natural ecosystems in stabilizing soil and preventing massive erosion, the loss of such habitat (for example, by drainage to convert land to agriculture) has deleterious effects on water quality both in the immediate vicinity of the wetland loss and downstream.

Opportunities for multiple benefits

A necessary step in reducing adverse impacts on fresh water, as well as on marine and other ecosystems, is to use water more efficiently. A fundamental strategy in sustainable water management, which can assist planners in achieving more efficient water use, is to integrate water management goals into physical, social, and economic planning—including agricultural management, overall land-use planning, forest resource utilization, and protection of coastal zones and marine environments from land-based activities.

Appropriate water-conservation strategies—such as rainwater conservation by terracing slopes and different means of water storage, including underground storage—will differ according to the characteristics of the region, and are particularly important in arid areas. Other potential measures include improvements in irrigation management, such as lining canals and using high-efficiency irrigation systems to prevent land degradation through

Terraced fields have permitted intensive agriculture on the same fields for centuries in parts of Asia.

salinization and waterlogging. Using treated wastewater for irrigation increases the freshwater available for other uses, including the maintenance of healthy aquatic ecosystems. Decreased, or more efficient, use of fertilizers in agriculture can reduce the need for expensive treatment of water from nearby water bodies to make it suitable for human use.

Efficient and economical water management need not be technologically challenging. One of the simplest strategies to improve both water supply management and water quality is the protection of watersheds through maintenance of naturally vegetated buffer strips along stream and river channels and around lakes. Wetland preservation is another important element of watershed protection. The resulting gains in water quality and natural water storage can reduce the need for, and therefore the costs of, water treatment and storage infrastructure downstream.

MEETING DEMANDS FOR ENERGY, INDUSTRIAL GOODS, AND EMPLOYMENT

The world's growing population, with its desire for a better quality of life, increasingly is seeking employment opportunities in the industrial and commercial sectors of the economy. The resulting growth in the formal economy will increase demand for energy. The outcome of the potential conflict between growing energy needs and major global environmental issues will be determined by decisions made on both aspects of energy management: demand and supply.

Providing energy, goods, and employment— Effects on global environmental issues

By far the most common way to satisfy needs for energy in modern societies is through burning fossil fuels such as coal, oil, and natural gas. Each year, this use of fossil fuels releases billions of tons of pollutants—particularly carbon dioxide—into the atmosphere (some 6 billion tons of carbon were released in 1990, 43 percent from coal, 39 percent

from oil, and 18 percent from natural gas). These emissions contribute to human-caused climate change. Changes in the climate system will in turn affect biodiversity and ecological systems, alterations that can feed back to the climate system through changes in albedo and the rates at which carbon and nitrogen cycle between the terrestrial biosphere and the atmosphere. Fossil fuel burning in the Northern Hemisphere also has resulted in large emissions of sulfate aerosols, which—by blocking some of the sun's radiation—slow the rate of increase in global surface temperature that otherwise would result from increasing concentrations of greenhouse gases. These sulfur compounds are major contributors to acidification of waters and soils.

Fossil fuel burning also results in the release of nitrogenous gases, some of which contribute to global warming. Other gases in this family affect air quality through chemical reactions in the atmosphere that result in the production of ozone—a primary component of smog in the lower atmosphere and a harmful substance to plants and human respiratory systems. These various types of nitrogenous compounds released during fossil fuel burning eventually wash out of the atmosphere and have resulted in substantial net increases in nitrogen loading of ecosystems. Highly industrialized regions, such as the eastern United States and western Europe, have experienced episodes of high nitrogen deposition in precipitation, thought to be another contributor (with sulfur compounds) to the regional acidification of surface waters.

The industrial sector is a major contributor to global and regional environmental problems, due to its high rates of natural resource use and pollution. Traditional industrial uses of materials are dissipative—the materials are degraded, dispersed, and lost to the economic system in the course of a single use. This sector is responsible for more than one-third of global CO_2 emissions from energy use, and contributes significantly to total emissions of other greenhouse gases. In fact, in 1990 industry accounted for almost half of global CO_2 releases (47 percent) when direct industrial consumption of energy and industrial uses of energy are combined.

Global industrial energy use is expected to rise 75 percent by the year 2050, and an increasing portion of the growth is expected to take place in developing countries. The growth of industrial activity in developing countries will be beneficial in terms of increased income and employment opportunities. However, it also represents potential increases in industrial contributions to global, regional, and local environmental problems through increases in greenhouse gas emissions, liquid and solid wastes, local air and water pollution, and resource consumption.

Effects of global environmental issues on energy use and supply, the production of goods, and employment

The effects of changes in the climate system on energy demand are expected to be relatively modest. If climate change results in shifts in seasonality and changes in temperature extremes, seasonal patterns of energy demand for heating and cooling may be altered in many regions. On the supply side, the acceleration of the hydrologic cycle that likely will occur with climate change, and the concurrent changes in cycles of precipitation and drought, will change the availability of hydropower and affect the extent of its use—relative to fossil fuel energy—at least on a regional basis. Production of biomass for energy also could be affected.

Industrial sector production and employment are relatively insulated from direct effects of changes in the climate system, loss of biodiversity, and other global environmental issues. To the extent that transportation networks depend on the use of rivers and inland waterways, the transportation of industrial goods to markets may be affected by changes in the hydrological cycle that result from climate change. There are even fewer direct links between the loss of biodiversity and effects on industrial productivity and employment. The conversion of natural habitat is not likely to result in significant increases in industrial production, since industrial growth is more likely to occur in already-urbanized landscapes with available supplies of energy, water, and labor. The sector's greatest threat from the loss of biodiversity stems from its reliance on diminishing supplies of wild genetic material for the production of agricultural products, medicines, and other products derived from natural sources.

Opportunities for multiple benefits

There are many technologies and practices for mitigating the adverse environmental impacts of this sector, some of which have multiple benefits—such as mitigating climate change (see box F), protecting biodiversity and water resources, and combating desertification. Some of these options might involve complex tradeoffs among different environmental impacts; for example, some options that improve regional environmental conditions may lead to higher GHG emissions or potential land-use conflicts. However, some technologies and practices have the potential to yield multiple environmental and socioeconomic benefits.

Technological advances and declining costs for energy from renewable sources offer new opportunities. In the long term, renewable energy sources can meet a major part of the world's demand for energy (see figure 22). Renewable energy sources that are used sustainably have little or no adverse environmental impact and could bring about sub-

Box F

Strategies for reducing greenhouse gas emissions

Residential, commercial, and institutional buildings
- Increase efficiency of building equipment (heating and cooling equipment, cooking, lighting, motors)
- Improve building thermal integrity (insulation and sealing, proper orientation)

Transportation
- Reduce vehicle energy intensity (change vehicle body/engine design, downsize vehicles)
- Switch to alternative energy sources (compressed natural gas, hydrogen or electricity from renewable sources)
- Improve urban transportation planning (public and non-motorized transport systems)
- Encourage telecommuting

Industry
- Use new or improved technologies and processes (reduce N_2O emissions from nylon production)
- Increase energy efficiency (more efficient lights, motors, and pumps)
- Cogeneration (combined heat and power, gas turbines/combined cycle, fuel cells)
- Material substitution/recycling/reuse

Energy supply
- Improve conversion and transmission efficiency
- Switch to low-carbon fuels (from coal and oil to natural gas)
- Decarbonize flue gases (scrubbing, coal gasification)
- Switch to renewable energy sources (biomass, wind energy) or nuclear power

Agriculture
- Increase C storage in agricultural soils (reduce tillage, increase permanent set-aside)
- Improve management of ruminant animals (increase feed digestibility, animal fertility)
- Prevent CH_4 emissions from animal wastes (use biogas generators)
- Increase efficiency of nitrogen fertilizer use

Forestry
- Slow deforestation
- Increase forestation/agroforestry
- Adopt substitution management practices (bio-electricity production from degraded lands, use sustainably-grown wood)

Solid waste and wastewater
- Reduce sources of solid waste (recycling, composting, incineration)
- Recover methane (from landfills, wastewater treatment plants)

Economic instruments
- Removal or strategic use of subsidies
- Domestic taxes
- Tradable permits/quotas
- Joint implementation

Traffic management in Santiago, Chile, involves both improved bus routing and expansion of the metro.

43

FIGURE 22

Energy supply — Sustained growth scenario

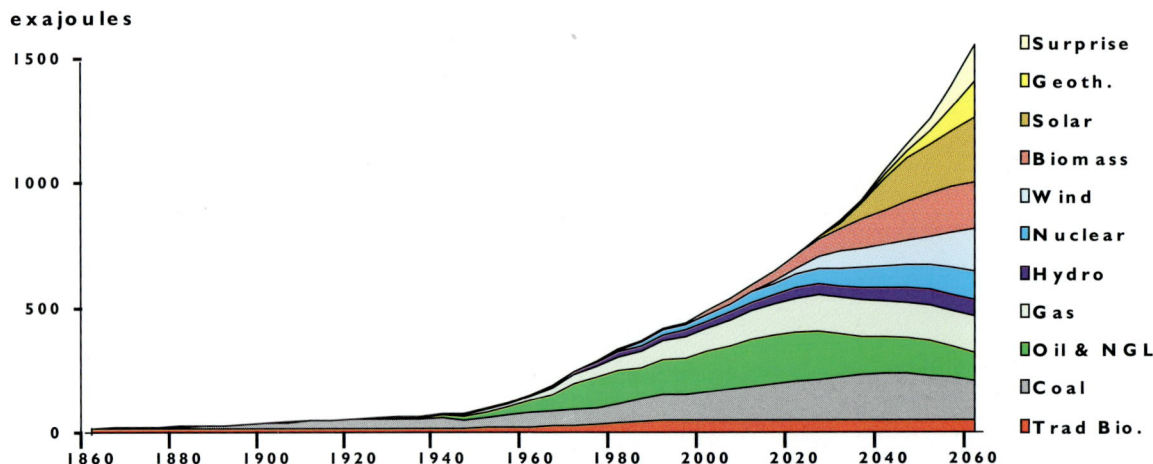

Source: Shell International Limited.

stantial reductions in adverse environmental impacts compared to fossil fuels; for example, by reducing emissions of particulates and associated human health impacts. Biomass can be used to produce electricity in a variety of conversion processes, including turbine technology, gasification, biogas production, and direct combustion (see box G). Applications of this energy source can vary in scale from rural villages to major urban supply systems. Further research and development will be required to bring some approaches to technical maturity and economical viability. There are also concerns about whether there will be enough land to meet the demand for increased food production and future bio-energy needs. Wind energy facilities, such as those for electricity production and water pumping, are commercially available and can be cost-competitive in some markets, although the range of costs is very wide. Solar energy options include photovoltaic (PV) and solar thermal technologies. Generally, solar energy does not have any direct, adverse environmental impacts, except in rare cases

of toxic pollution in the manufacture, use, and disposal of systems. Many applications are already cost-competitive as stand-alone systems in areas remote from electrical grids.

Over the past decades energy efficiency has been increasing, especially in the more industrialized countries. These improvements have been achieved through a wide range of measures, such as more efficient use of raw materials, use of combined heat and power systems, better systems coordination within and among firms, and use of more efficient industrial processes. These improvements have led to significant improvements in local and regional environmental quality, and to lower-cost production. Great potential exists to extend the use of such technologies and practices within developed as well as less industrialized countries.

A number of available technologies can increase the efficiency of power production, making it possible to improve the present world average of about 30 percent efficiency to more than 60 percent efficiency in the long term, reducing the need

Box G

Guidance for "win-win" projects—Biomass for energy

Sustainably harvesting biomass for energy requires ecologically sound management and the use of best management practices. Some specific suggestions for ensuring that biomass-for-energy projects are successful and sustainable over the long term are listed below.

Use sustainable management practices:
- Produce a mix of crops, where sites and markets allow, diversifying the landscape and spreading risk. Give preference to native species and hybrid species in the same genus.
- Encourage perennial energy crops that enhance nutrient cycling and retention of nutrients on site.
- Rotate crops or species to reduce nutrient depletion or buildup of pests where perennial crops are not feasible.
- Add fertilizers only as required to meet plant uptake requirements.
- Minimize total chemical-pesticide inputs by using integrated pest management practices.
- When harvesting forest or agricultural residues, leave sufficient material on the forest floor/field to control erosion and ensure adequate nutrients for future vegetation. Where appropriate, return ash and processing residues from biomass conversion facilities to the land as soil amendments.

Minimize negative impacts on habitat and biodiversity:
- Harvesting activities should incorporate regeneration or replanting practices that will maintain indigenous biodiversity levels (for example, leave sufficient numbers of large standing trees that are dead or dying to provide habitat).
- Minimize fragmentation and improve overall habitat quality for native species.
- Match native species types as much as possible (for example, perennial grasses in prairie regions), and emulate natural vegetation patterns and functions.
- Encourage genetic and species diversity of energy crop plantings.
- Sites selected to grow energy crops should primarily be cropland; avoid critical habitat sites.
- Schedule field operations to minimize disturbance during critical periods of animals' life cycles (nesting, winter cover).
- Delineate buffer zones (including corridors) for the protection of wildlife habitat.

Minimize negative impacts on soils and water:
- Design harvesting schedules to avoid soil compaction, erosion.
- Manage energy crops to increase soil organic matter content.
- Use conservation tillage practices where applicable.
- Delineate buffer zones for the protection of water.

Consider climate issues:
- In species selection, consider the ability of crops to sequester significant amounts of carbon through roots and other material left on site.

Seek public acceptance:
- Incorporate aesthetic and cultural values when planning at the regional level, to ensure long-term acceptance of a new industry.

for additional energy generation and its associated environmental costs. Improving the efficiency of energy production and conversion is generally a win-win strategy. At relatively low cost, the potential for energy efficiency improvement is large and can result in reduced environmental impacts at all scales. A number of advanced and new technologies—ranging from high-temperature gas turbines to fuel cells—promise even higher efficiencies in the production and conversion of fossil fuels. Existing

FIGURE 23

The total industrial ecology cycle

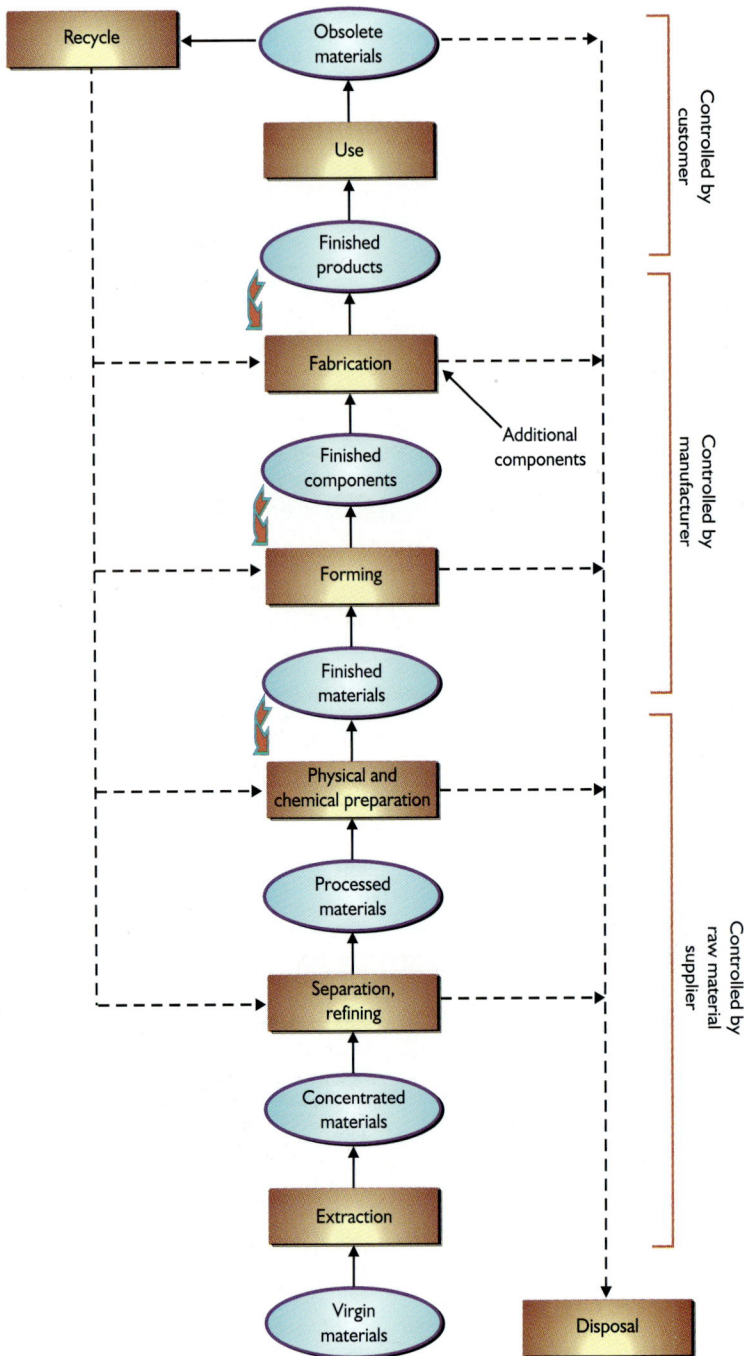

Source: T. E. Graedel and B. R. Allenby. 1995. *Industrial Ecology*, Prentice Hall.

technologies to reduce the environmental impacts of energy production include more efficient methods of energy production, and switching to fossil fuels with lower carbon emissions—such as from coal to oil or natural gas, or from oil to natural gas. Another possible option in some parts of the world is switching to nuclear energy.

Efficiency improvements and energy conservation in end-use equipment are equally important. Significant reductions in energy use in buildings, for example, can be achieved through improvements in building design, such as reduction of heat-transfer (through the use of energy-efficient windows) and proper building orientation to reduce the need for heating and cooling. Other measures to reduce energy needs in buildings and improve environmental quality include: urban design and land-use planning; installing efficient district heating and cooling systems; ensuring correct installation, operation, and sizing of equipment; and using building energy management systems.

Improvements in energy efficiency can be achieved in the transport sector through a variety of technical and social options, including improved gas mileage, higher occupancy rates per vehicle, use of public transportation, and improved traffic management and urban transport system planning. Encouraging the use of bicycles and other non-motorized transport and improving telecommunications can reduce transport energy requirements as well as adverse environmental impacts.

Further benefits can be achieved through the adoption of "industrial ecology" practices, which are based on maximizing industrial efficiency and minimizing waste and undesirable byproducts released into the environment (see figure 23). This approach aims to optimize the total industrial material cycle—from virgin material to finished product to the ultimate disposal of waste (see box H).

Widespread adoption of modern industrial ecology and clean production could ease a number of global, regional, and local environmental problems. Global environmental benefits include reduced emissions of greenhouse gases and ozone-depleting substances, reduced introduction of persistent organic pollutants into the environment, and reduced demand for primary resources, resulting in diminished pressure on natural ecosystems and reduced loss of species diversity. Regional and local benefits include improvements in surface and groundwater quality, reductions in urban air pollution, reduced deposition of acid and toxic compounds, and slower rates of resource depletion and exhaustion of landfills.

Widespread adoption of energy efficient and clean production practices will not be possible without overcoming a number of barriers. Low fuel

---

Box H

Guidance for "win-win" projects—Industrial ecology

The environmental performance of industry can be improved by applying models of the biophysical environment to industrial production. One emerging concept for the development of industrial ecology principles is the Eco-Industrial Park (EIP): communities of manufacturing and service businesses that aim to enhance their environmental and economic performance through collaboration in managing environmental issues and resources—including energy, water, and materials. Components of this approach include new or retrofitted design of infrastructure and plants, pollution prevention, and energy efficiency. Strategies for designing successful industrial parks include:

Integration into Natural Systems
- Design the EIP in harmony with the characteristics and constraints of local ecosystems
- Minimize contributions to global environmental impacts, such as greenhouse gas emissions

Energy Systems
- Maximize energy efficiency through facility design or rehabilitation, co-generation, and energy cascading
- Achieve higher efficiency through inter-plant energy flows
- Use renewable sources extensively

Materials Flows and "Waste" Management
- Emphasize pollution prevention, especially with toxics
- Ensure maximum re-use and recycling of materials among EIP businesses
- Reduce toxic materials risks through integrated site-level waste treatment
- Link the EIP to companies in the surrounding region as consumers and generators of usable byproducts via resource exchanges and recycling networks

Water
- Design water flows to conserve resources and reduce pollution through strategies similar to those described for energy and materials

Effective EIP Management
- Maintain a mix of companies needed to best use each other's by-products
- Support improvement in environmental performance for individual companies and the park as a whole
- Operate a site-wide information system that supports inter-company communications, informs members of local environmental conditions, and provides feedback on EIP performance

Construction/Rehabilitation
- New construction or rehabilitation of existing buildings should follow best environmental practices in materials selection and building technology, recycling or reuse of materials and consideration of lifecycle environmental implications of materials and technologies.

prices, for example, provide little incentive to invest in high-efficiency energy systems, unless an investment can bring dramatic cost reductions in a short time. Increased adoption of industrial ecology would necessitate extensive education in the business sector about the benefits of these practices, and a shift in corporate culture to a new way of doing business.

HEALTH AND SECURITY OF POPULATIONS

Among the primary goals of any society is the protection of the physical security, health, and economic well-being of its members. The links between these issues and global environmental changes are generally poorly understood. Most people are only vaguely aware of the environmental impacts of economic development and personal consumption, and often seem to consider the impacts trivial in comparison to the benefits. In fact, our health and well-being rest on an environmental platform and depend particularly on the sustained functioning of ecological systems. As we continue to erode that platform, we put our future and that of our children increasingly at risk. One of the fundamental reasons for minimizing environmental pollution and sustaining Earth system processes is to safeguard human health. Another important—though less understood—reason is to avoid conflicts over scarce resources, for example water resources in regions such as the Middle East.

Health

The focus of concern over environmental hazards to human health has traditionally been in relation to chemical and microbial contamination of air, water, soil, or food. While these remain important issues, we must now also address the larger-scale, sometime more diffuse, hazards to human health posed by changes in the planet's biophysical systems. These hazards include climate change, stratospheric ozone depletion, unsustainable use of water supplies, and fragmentation of ecological systems, all of which have a bearing on food yields and the range and transmission of infectious diseases. These newer hazards refer not just to local, remediable, environmental agents, but to more profound changes in life-supporting natural systems.

The advent of human-caused climate change, depletion of stratospheric ozone, land degradation, biodiversity loss, and the dissemination of persistent toxic chemicals all increase risks to human health. The health of human populations is affected by a wide range of environmental conditions and ecological services, including air and water quality, food production and quality, fluctuations in the ecology of pests and infectious pathogens, and the predictability of weather patterns. In the longer term, patterns of human health and disease will be affected by changes in the geography of infectious (especially insect-borne) diseases, changes in regional food yields on land and at sea, changes in the habitability of coastal zones and the occurrence of extreme weather events, and the social-demographic consequences of rapid urbanization.

It is anticipated that most of the impacts of global environmental issues on human health would be adverse. Some would occur via relatively direct pathways (for example, deaths from heat waves and from extreme weather events); others would occur via indirect pathways (such as changes in the range of vector-borne diseases). Some impacts would be deferred in time and would occur on a larger scale than most other environmental health impacts with which we are familiar. Populations with different levels of natural, technical, and social resources would differ in their vulnerability. Such vulnerability, due to crowding, food insecurity, local and regional environmental degradation, and perturbed ecosystems, already exists in many locations.

Direct effects could include an increase in cardiorespiratory mortality and illness from heat waves. Studies in selected urban populations in North America, North Africa, and East Asia indicate that the number of heat-related deaths would increase several-fold in response to future climate, as modeled by two general circulation models for 2050.

Another example of an increased health risk attributable to large-scale environmental change is the recent shifts in patterns of some infectious diseases (see figure 24). For example, recent agricultural expansion into previously forested areas in South America has resulted in new viral hemorrhagic fevers, spread among humans by rodents or mosquitoes. Although the building of large dams in Egypt and Senegal brought economic benefits, the reservoirs created by the dams also provided breeding grounds for disease vectors, resulting in increases in Rift Valley fever and schistosomiasis. Regional warming has been associated with malaria moving to higher altitudes in eastern Africa over the past two decades. Finally, the rapid dissemination of cholera in coastal Peruvian populations in 1991 seems likely to have been due to the widespread presence of cholera bacterium in the local fish catch, following the increase in coastal algal blooms (a natural reservoir for the cholera bacterium) that were present in the region, due to the combination of coastal-water warming and nutrient-rich wastewater runoff.

Malaria provides an instructive example of an important vector-borne infectious disease that can be influenced by various types of global environmental change. Malaria currently causes around 350 million new infections annually (including 2 millions deaths), predominately in tropical countries.

FIGURE 24
Vector-borne diseases

Disease	Vector	Population at risk (millions)	Present distribution	Likelihood of altered distribution with warming
Malaria	mosquito	2,100	(sub)tropics	✓✓✓
Schistosomiasis	water snail	600	(sub)tropics	✓✓
Filariasis	mosquito	900	(sub)tropics	✓
Onchocerciasis (river blindness)	black fly	90	Africa/Latin America	✓
African trypanosomiasis (sleeping sickness)	tsetse fly	50	tropical Africa	✓
Dengue	mosquito	unavailable	tropics	✓✓
Yellow fever	mosquito	unavailable	tropical South America & Africa	✓

Likely ✓
Very likely ✓✓
Highly likely ✓✓✓

Source: WHO, as cited in Stone (1995).

The rapid clearing of forests in tropical and subtropical regions, especially when cleared for agriculture, can result in increases of habitat suitable for a variety of disease vectors, especially mosquitoes that transmit malaria. In some settings, however, forest clearance may reduce the habitat of the principal local species of mosquito that transmits malaria. Simultaneously, the opening up of cleared land provides the opportunity for large-scale migration and colonization of these regions by human populations that may lack resistance to malaria and thus provide dramatic increases in host availability. The net result is an increase in transmission rates and population-level morbidity, due almost entirely to land-use change.

Malaria has historically been a disease of tropical, sub-tropical, and warm temperate climates. Its current geographic distribution represents a balance between the climatic requirements of malaria-carrying mosquitoes and the ability of various societies to control the insects through the use of pesticides and other control measures. Under conditions of climate change, the potential range of mosquitoes and of the malaria parasite will extend to higher latitudes and higher altitudes—including into regions with no previous history of, and limited defenses against, malaria. Climate-related increases in malaria incidence have been projected to be as high as 50 to 80 million additional cases annually, primarily in tropical, subtropical, and less well-protected temperate zone populations.

The health risks of stratospheric ozone depletion are well known. Increased exposure to UV-B radiation can result in increases in melanoma and non-melanoma skin cancer and cataract formation. According to the most recent ozone assessment (1998), for a "European" population living around 45 degrees North, there will be an excess incidence of skin cancers peaking at around 5 percent during the third quarter of the coming century, entailing an extra 100 cases/million per year (vs. current background of 2000 cases/million per year), assuming rates and levels of ozone depletion consistent with implementation of the Copenhagen amendments to the Montreal Protocol. There is some evidence that increased exposure to UV-B radiation can also result in decreased immune system performance, which would increase susceptibility to infectious diseases and perhaps to certain cancers.

National Security

Protection of national security has always been one of the most basic functions of national government. Security against conflict and aggression is a precondition for the effective provision of other human needs. The establishment of a strong military and effective international security alliances has historically been the sole focus of government policies for providing that security. We are just beginning to understand the crucial links between national security and the environment. Some of these links are so strong that in some regions of the world, environmental concerns could logically be considered national security issues. Some national governments have established special groups solely to monitor environmental trends, which they contend could lead to conflict in some regions.

Global environmental issues can have a major influence on the security of nations because they may exacerbate or ameliorate the conditions for conflict. In many regions of the world, including the Middle East and Africa, disputes over access to freshwater resources have exacerbated existing conflicts. Scarcity of water resources is one of the important factors in disputes between Israel and the Palestinians. Senior officials in both Israel and Egypt have warned that if water-sharing arrangements are unsuccessful, war could result. Growing demands for fresh water will increase the risk of conflicts, and changes in precipitation patterns and temperature as a result of climate change can shift the locations of such conflicts to areas that previously may have had sufficient water resources.

The world has seen a steady stream of conflicts over the increasingly depleted stocks of fish in the oceans beyond territorial waters. Some have involved loss of life, clashes between coast guard and naval vessels from different nations, and the seizure of one country's fishing boats by other countries. Even nations that are close allies have had serious disputes over this shrinking resource.

Similarly, if productivity is reduced due to a changing climate, changing water availability, or depletion of natural resources, local populations may be driven to migrate to more productive areas.

Human migrations stemming from environmental degradation already involve millions of displaced people—sometimes referred to as "environmental refugees." The number of these refugees could increase dramatically in coming decades with changes in climate and sea level (see figure 25). For example, studies using a projected one-meter rise in sea level indicate that large numbers of people may be affected—for example, about 70 million each in China and Bangladesh (see figure 7). In these studies, many nations lost financial capital greater than 10 percent of their gross domestic product. The vulnerability of the populations of these countries is illustrated by recent flooding of agricultural land and proximate human settlements. On low-lying islands and atolls, retreat away from the coast is rarely an option, and as a result, migration and resettlement outside current national boundaries may be necessary.

FIGURE 25

People at risk from a 44 cm sea-level rise by the 2080s, assuming 1990s level of flood protection

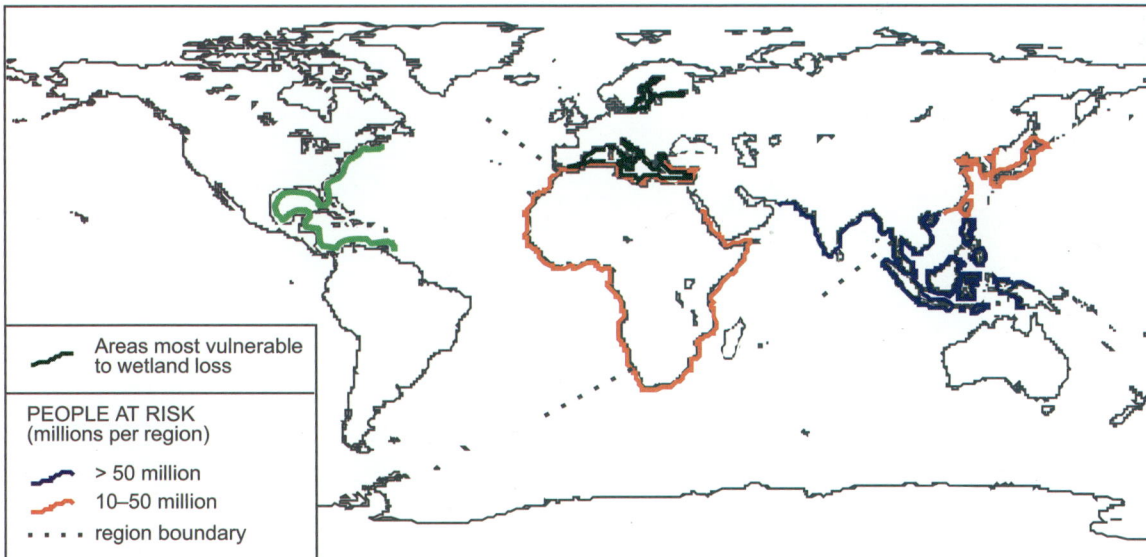

Areas most vulnerable to wetland loss

PEOPLE AT RISK
(millions per region)

> 50 million
10–50 million
. . . . region boundary

Source: R. Nicholls, Middlesex University in the U.K. Meteorological Office. 1997. *Climate Change and Its Impacts: A Global Perspective.* Brittanic Crown Copyright.

Part IV

POLICIES FOR LINKING HUMAN AND ENVIRONMENTAL NEEDS

THE WORLD'S EXPERIENCE since the 1992 United Nations Conference on Environment and Development (UNCED)—the Rio Earth Summit— suggests cautious optimism about the potential for effective, cost-efficient environmental reform at the national level. Although necessary financial resources are often limited, and major institutional issues need to be resolved, many of the approaches being used to address national environmental problems also can be used by countries to respond creatively to globally linked environmental issues.

Effective policy implementation that links global environmental issues and sustainable development has four requirements:

■ Scientific understanding of the nature of the links among environmental issues and their relationship to meeting human needs, to facilitate the balancing of competing needs and the identification of strategies that capture as many benefits as possible

■ Identification of innovative combinations of policies that are effective and cost-efficient and that encourage the public and private sectors to work together

■ Political will and public commitment (from both individuals and the private sector) to seriously address global environmental issues, including setting realistic goals and identifying creative paths for achieving them

■ Improved coordination among the national and international institutions charged with developing and encouraging adoption of policies and measures to meet human needs, without undermining the environmental foundation for development.

Many countries are making progress toward reducing the rate of resource degradation, improving local and regional air and water quality, and supplying growing populations with adequate food and fiber. In the industrialized world and some developing countries, energy efficiency—the ratio of usable energy output to primary energy input—is improving in many sectors of the economy. Likewise, the intensity of consumption—the amount of inputs used in the production of any product—of key resources such as water, land, and materials is falling. These favorable trends—using less energy and fewer inputs to provide each person with the goods and services that they demand—benefit the environment, and in recent years have been observed in both developed and developing countries. As a result, some countries in the developing world have less environmental degradation than that experienced by industrialized countries when they were at a similar stage of economic development.

However, many encouraging trends within countries have been more than offset by increases in total demand for resources stemming from the combined effects of growth in income and rapid rises in population. The net impact on the environment, therefore, is often negative. For example, although the number of urban dwellers in developing countries with access to adequate water increased by about 80 per cent during the 1980s, these gains were overshadowed by rapid urban population growth, so that at least 220 million urban dwellers still lack access to clean drinking water. Similarly, recent improvements in energy intensity have been overwhelmed by increasing total demands for energy, and fossil fuel emissions have continued to grow.

A second trend that has slowed progress in addressing global environmental issues is a general lack of implementation of international conventions and agreements. For example, little action has been

Rapid population growth, especially in the world's major cities, is affecting local and global environments.

taken to implement the agreements reached at the Rio Earth Summit in 1992. The funds that governments make available and the political will to work toward halting further global environmental degradation are widely acknowledged to be inadequate. Progress also is hampered by institutional weaknesses, insufficient human resources, inadequate enforcement of environmental standards and other regulations, market barriers, a lack of public understanding and support for efforts to address environmental issues, and poor coordination across environmental management regimes and international conventions. Another important condition for change is the existence of affordable alternatives, always a major issue in a world of limited budgetary resources.

In addition, the focus of many nations remains on immediate local and national issues, while less attention is paid to what are perceived as global and long-term environmental problems (even though global problems are created by national actions and have implications at the local level). One exception is the issue of ozone depletion. As a result of a series of international agreements to phase out the use of ozone-depleting substances, the ozone layer is expected to recover to pre-1970 levels by the middle of the next century. The progress in this case was possible for several reasons: the cause of ozone depletion was well understood and involved a limited number of producers of targeted substances, governments and industry broadly agreed on necessary steps for solving the problem, the costs of alternatives were reasonable, and governments were willing to create a trust fund to help developing countries meet their obligations under the agreements. For many of the other global environmental issues discussed in this report, these conditions do not exist.

These two trends—growth that overwhelms reductions in environmental impacts per unit of output, and inadequate implementation of existing agreements—result in continued global environmental degradation. The challenges to policymakers, therefore, are to accelerate positive environmental trends while removing the obstacles to further progress.

There is good news, however. Growing awareness of the links among global environmental issues offers the possibility of devising policies that can meet both local and global needs, and that produce multiple benefits. Many technologies and practices exist that can help meet several important social and economic goals simultaneously, while avoiding environmental problems. These goals include: reducing poverty, expanding food production, providing energy services, improving the conditions of human settlements, and avoiding problems that put burdens on future generations. One example is growing trees and other plants to produce fuel from renewable sources. The substitution of such modern plantation biomass sources for fossil fuels can reduce energy-related greenhouse gas emissions, and also can have positive impacts on biodiversity and local air and water quality. Successful establishment of ecologically and economically sound biomass plantations is an exciting example of a win-

win scenario in which the local, national, and global environment and economies benefit.

Biomass plantations are increasingly being used to produce energy from renewable sources.

Policies that yield multiple benefits need to avoid a single issue and/or sectoral focus that seeks to attain only one goal or objective. A single issue focus creates the potential for unproductive competition among environmental and developmental goals, setting the stage for future conflicts among policies and projects. Solving environmental problems and moving to more sustainable forms of development involves tradeoffs and the realization that focusing on only one objective at the expense of others will most likely be counterproductive in the long term. For example, efforts to maximize food production through agricultural intensification initially boosted yields. But some of these gains were soon eroded as a result of declines in soil and water quality, requiring ever larger inputs of fertilizers and pesticides to maintain production. Thus practical solutions often require balancing competing needs, and it is important to make pragmatic choices that capture as many benefits as possible, and not to delay action while waiting for a "perfect" solution.

55

One of the major achievements of recent international environmental agreements and institutions has been the effective incorporation of leading edge scientific thought and research into the design of appropriate public policies and international agreements. Through such mechanisms as the Intergovernmental Panel on Climate Change and the Global Biodiversity Assessment, science has been brought to bear on important policy issues. However, like the agreements themselves, this scientific input has given relatively little attention to the interlinkages among the various institutions and issues. This calls for a more integrative assessment process for selected scientific issues, a process that can highlight the linkages between questions relevant to decisionmakers addressing climate, biodiversity, desertification, and forest issues. Redundancy would be avoided by developing assessment processes and institutions that meet the needs of multiple institutions, and the opportunity for identifying and benefiting from win-win solutions would be enhanced.

New Approaches to Policymaking

Policymakers face a major challenge in improving environmental management, but exciting opportunities exist to take advantage of global interlinkages, potential synergies between various approaches, and increasing roles for both the public and private sectors. In the past, policies to address environmental problems generally have involved regulations (the "command and control" approach). Experience has shown, however, that desired changes often can be made more effectively by using a combination of different types of policies and with the cooperation of the public and private sectors. For example, the successful campaign to reduce the production and use of ozone-depleting substances has combined the use of direct regulations (such as bans on certain chemicals) with market incentives and subsidies to help ease the transition to alternative technologies.

The foundation for successful implementation of innovative policies is the establishment of what might be termed "basic enabling conditions" for effective social, political, and economic decisionmaking. These conditions are necessary for successful governance and are important for creating incentives and information required for long-term, sustainable management of resources. Governments must work with the private sector and civic groups to establish these basic enabling conditions and to initiate targeted policy interventions to promote desired environmental changes (see box I).

Building on these basic enabling conditions, governments can use many different types of policies to improve the management of environmental resources (see figure 26). These interventions can be grouped into three broad categories, depending on their basic approach to influencing decisionmaking and resource use:

- *Command and control strategies*, including establishment and enforcement of regulations, standards, product bans, and quotas/permits
- *Market-based interventions*, including restructuring economic incentives (removing pre-existing market distortions such as subsidies), correcting market failures (taxes or other charges to reflect social and environmental costs associated with resource use), and creating markets through the use of tradable permits

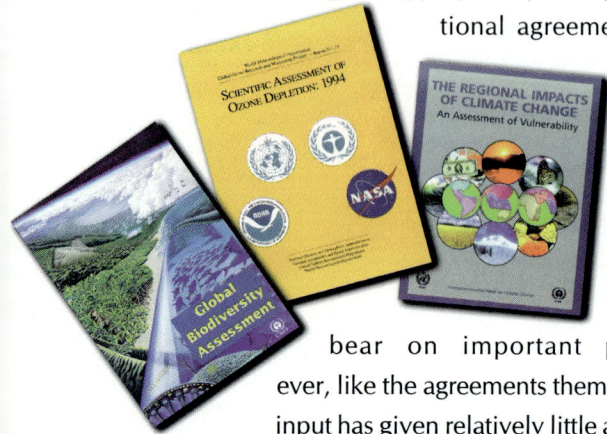

Box I

Enabling conditions for effective policy change

The combination of several important enabling conditions can help create a political climate suitable for effective policy change:

Proper incentive systems

A key role of government is to ensure that proper incentive systems are in place to encourage the effective implementation of policies that recognize global linkages among environmental issues and human needs. Changes in the fiscal, legal, liability, or property-rights systems may be needed to promote policy implementation. For example, the establishment of well-defined, exclusive, secure, enforceable, and legally transferable property rights provides a powerful incentive for long-term sustainable management of resources. Granting some use rights also may lead to improved resource management by giving the users of a resource a stake in protecting it for potential future use. Along with private property rights, public property rights are important and can, for example, encourage sustainable management of national marine fisheries. Other examples of incentive systems are the legal and infrastructure systems for creating markets for global public goods, such as carbon trading.

Strong legal frameworks

Strengthening environmental codes and laws is an important step toward improving the implementation of policies. Environmental regulations in most countries are far from adequate to ensure the sustainable management of the Earth's resources. Effective implementation of environmental policies requires appropriate institutions (a Ministry of the Environment or a National Council for Sustainable Development); comprehensive legislation to protect water and air quality, ecosystems, and other environmental systems; adequate human and financial resources; and infrastructure to allow compliance monitoring.

Public participation

Nearly all of the global conventions and statements discussed in this report reflect the importance of public awareness and participation in addressing global environmental issues. Participation of stakeholders in setting priorities, choosing response options, and implementing policies can ensure informed decisionmaking and strengthen ownership of projects, thereby increasing the likelihood that policies will meet their objectives.

Cooperation with the private sector

Since public resources alone are not adequate to meet global objectives, the private sector has a crucial role to play in implementing change. Whereas the various international development banks invest about US$50 billion per year in developing countries, annual private international capital flows are about five times this amount. Even larger amounts are invested locally—by public and private investors—each year within the developing world. These investment resources represent an important opportunity to implement policies designed to achieve multiple benefits.

Technological capacity

Research, development, and demonstration programs to foster the creation of new technologies and encourage their diffusion into the marketplace are critical and currently underfunded. It is essential to develop collaborative approaches between government, industry, and academia and between developed and developing countries.

Financial and institutional capacity

Successful policy implementation assumes widespread human, institutional, and financial capacity. Such capacity is important for facilitating and financing the transfer of environmentally-sound technologies, knowledge, and experience; strengthening institutional capacities for research and development; and program implementation. The necessary capacity is lacking in many developing countries.

Information for assessment and monitoring

If countries are to successfully address globally linked environmental problems, it is necessary to understand the rate and pace of change in various environmental variables and the links between different systems. Accordingly, integrative scientific assessments are crucial to highlighting the links between environmental systems; and with this information indicators can be developed to monitor progress through the change of important environmental variables. In recent years there has been progress in indicator development at both the national and international levels.

FIGURE 26

The policy matrix

		USING MARKETS (Subsidy reduction, taxes, user fees, performance bonds, targeted subsidies)	**CREATING MARKETS** (Property rights and decentralization, tradable permits, international offset systems)	**ENVIRONMENTAL REGULATIONS** (Standards, bans, quotas)	**ENGAGING THE PUBLIC** (Information disclosure, public participation)
Resource Management	WATER				
	FISHERIES				
	LAND MANAGEMENT				
	FORESTS				
	SUSTAINABLE AGRICULTURE				
	BIODIVERSITY/ PROT. AREAS				
Pollution Control	MINERALS				
	AIR POLLUTION				
	WATER POLLUTION				
	SOLID WASTE				
	HAZARDOUS WASTE				

Source: World Bank. 1997. *Five Years after Rio: Innovations in Environmental Policy.* Washington, D.C.

■ *Voluntary agreements* with public involvement, including voluntary agreements between polluters and/or resource users and regulators on permissible levels of pollution, and providing information to the public to help promote monitoring and compliance with agreed-upon plans of action.

Public participation and involvement are powerful forces for improved environmental management.

WORLD BANK

In addition potential exists for promoting more responsible global stewardship of environmental resources by improving coordination among the international environmental conventions. Possible approaches include: coordination among the international conventions themselves, and better coordination and communication among the country-level bodies that develop national inputs (national action plans, reports, or inventories) and policy positions for international negotiations on convention implementation.

Boxes J, M, and Q describe major categories of environmental policies and present examples of innovative policymaking that takes into account environmental linkages and meets multiple goals. Each of the three major types of policies has strengths and weaknesses, but they often can be used effectively in combination.

COMMAND AND CONTROL

The most direct way to influence environmental decisionmaking and resource use is to dictate standards (pollution emission rates) or the use of a specific technology (catalytic converters for cars or certain types of scrubbers for power plants), or to specify the desired outcome (maximum pollution levels for air or water). This approach is commonly referred to as "command and control " (CAC) policy, and includes the use of regulations, laws, and standards (see box J). Environmental laws worldwide mandate or limit certain practices or behavior—such as bans on the use of certain pesticides, limits on resource use or pollutant emissions, and mandatory energy efficiency or emissions standards. The idea of CAC is embedded in most global conventions and their associated protocols. All of the environmental conventions encourage the use of national regulatory measures, either by recommending the passage of general environmental legislation or by mandating specific measures (targeted reductions in the production and consumption of ozone-depleting substances; compliance with specified harvest levels for fish or trees).

Command and control policies are sometimes the only effective way of attaining certain environmental goals, such as regulating the use of very sensitive ecological areas or eliminating the use of extremely long-lived and toxic compounds.

Although CAC policies allow governments to set specific standards, achieving results often is costly. Because they deny different users or firms the flexibility to respond in the most cost-effective manner, command and control policies can miss important opportunities for cost savings and for achieving multiple benefits. To help reduce the costs of regulatory approaches, CAC policies increasingly

Box J

Policy instruments for improved environmental management—Command and control

Basic structure. This classic approach to environmental management relies on mandating certain practices or behavior (such as setting limits on the release of pollutants into the environment, harvesting of natural resources, or other activities with environmental impacts).

Examples:
- Bans on particular practices or on the use of certain products (for example, prohibiting the use of leaded gas)
- Non-tradable quotas or limits on resource use or pollutant emissions (emissions standards for air or water pollutants)
- Mandatory energy efficiency or emissions standards that cover a class of products or practices (fuel efficiency requirements for new cars).

Comments:
- Provide greater certainty in environmental results than market-based measures
- Afford less flexibility and thus have higher economic costs than more flexible approaches (such as voluntary compliance, market-based instruments)
- Require monitoring and enforcement, which can increase costs
- Are often combined with other instruments (such as trading of quotas or permits, pollution charges, or initiatives to encourage public involvement).

Command and control policies are commonly used to control pollution from major industries.

Box K

A mixed approach—The use of standards and fees to control palm-oil industry effluent in Malaysia

Creative policymaking often combines several different policy approaches to reach a desired goal. For example, to control water pollution from oil palm mills, the government of Malaysia has successfully implemented a combination of policies based on a licensing system—consisting of both effluent standards and charges—designed to reduce effluents over time. Four stages of progressively stringent effluent standards were set and enforced. Initially, a year was allowed for palm oil mills to install treatment facilities, after which they were required to progressively reduce their wastewater discharges. In addition to developing the pollutant standards, the Malaysian government levies effluent charges based on the volume of each mill's discharge. These charges have been increased annually. Finally, polluters are required to pay an annual license-processing fee; mills that have succeeded in developing technologies to reduce discharges are charged at a lower rate. As a result of this combination of standards, fees, and incentives, the palm oil industry has made steady progress toward meeting its targets. Between 1978 and 1989, despite a 93 percent increase in the number of palm oil mills and a three-fold increase in the production of crude palm oil, effluent loads released to public water bodies fell from 563 tons per day in 1978 to 5 tons per day in 1989. These pollution reductions were accomplished without affecting the competitiveness of the Malaysian palm oil industry.

Oil palm fruit ready for harvesting.

Box L

Quotas and charges for managing irrigation water use in Israel

Efforts to allocate scarce resources can benefit from a mix of policy instruments. By combining annual allocations for water with water charges, Israel has achieved remarkable efficiencies in the use of irrigation water. Under this system, irrigation water is allotted to licensed farmers based on an annual quota. Each farmer's quota is based on the area cultivated, the crop mix, and the water requirements of each crop. This allocation system provides an incentive for water efficiency, since farmers must sustain their farms on the allocated volume, and wasteful practices may force them to reduce their irrigated area or pay penalties for over-consumption. Charges for irrigation water are based on a progressive block rate structure, and consumption above the allocated limit is charged at a fixed rate per cubic meter. Prices also are indexed to seasonal conditions: A 40 percent premium is charged during peak irrigation months to cover the higher per unit energy demands for pumping that result from greater hydraulic losses in overloaded pipelines. This combination of policies has resulted in a steady decline in Israel's average water application rate per hectare and a notable increase in irrigation efficiency. Between 1951 and 1985, water use per hectare rates fell 36 percent, which meant that even though the area under irrigation increased in this period by 380 percent, water use for irrigation increased by only 200 percent.

have been combined with other instruments that rely on markets and economic signals (pollution charges, trading of permits or quotas—see boxes K and L). In these cases, setting limits on discharges of pollutants is a prerequisite to establishing markets for trading emissions rights.

Some countries are wary of setting strict environmental standards for fear of becoming less competitive internationally. For example, it has been speculated that unequal environmental standards could provide incentives for businesses to locate in countries with weak standards and thus reduce their pollution-control costs. The concentration of heavily polluting industries in countries with weaker standards could lead to environmental degradation in these countries, and would be economically harmful to the countries that lose industries. Large-scale industry movements also could affect trade balances and provide incentives for countries to implement compensatory trade measures. Empirical evidence, however, suggests that this so-called "race to the bottom" rarely happens; environmental standards appear to play only a minor role in location decisions for most industries. In addition, the General Agreement on Tariffs and Trade (GATT) warns against the use of unilateral trade measures to offset the competitive effects of different environmental standards.

The use of command and control approaches is well understood, and many governments are comfortable with this strategy. There is a growing realization, however, that relying on CAC often imposes excessive costs on an economy, and that monitoring and enforcement of these measures may exceed the regulatory capacity of many countries.

MARKET-BASED INTERVENTIONS

As global markets become increasingly important, the relative power of public institutions to dictate standards wanes. Governments have a powerful set of alternatives to traditional command and control policies in the form of market-based interventions, including subsidy reduction and elimination, targeted subsidies, taxes and fees, creation of markets for quotas or permits, and deposit-refund or performance bond systems (see box M). Such interventions use the marketplace to send signals of scarcity and opportunity costs, allowing individuals and firms to make informed decisions.

Box M

Policy instruments for improved environmental management — Market-based instruments

Basic structure. These approaches use price signals to affect economic decisions by producers and consumers.

Examples:
- Reduction/elimination of subsidies that artificially lower the price of scarce natural resources (water, fossil fuels)
- Targeted subsidies to encourage the use of environmentally friendly products (renewable energy sources, high-efficiency appliances)
- Taxes and fees (pollution charges)
- Creation of markets for tradable quotas or permits (for pollutant emissions)
- Deposit-refund or performance bond systems (for bottles or batteries).

Comments:
- Elimination of market distortions (subsidies) can slow demand growth (by encouraging resource conservation, improved efficiency, and substitution) and expand supply (through recycling, exploration, imports, and development of substitutes).
- Taxes and user fees can be used to make prices reflect the true costs of resource use to society, including the damages or costs that may result from emissions, release of effluents, or resource depletion. These so-called "full cost prices" are often difficult to estimate precisely.
- Allow private decisionmakers greater flexibility (which generally reduces costs).
- Have potential to yield fiscal benefits for governments, either by reducing costs (subsidy elimination) or raising revenues (taxes or fees).

The role of prices and the market are increasingly important for improved environmental management. Official development lending accounts for less than one-fifth of the annual total of international capital flows. Unless private sources of capital invest in sustainable development projects and programs, there is little hope of turning around many negative environmental trends. Strong strategic partnerships among governments, nongovernment organizations, the private sector and financial institutions—including development banks and private banks—can enable societies to respond effectively to market signals.

The importance of market-based instruments is increasingly recognized by global conventions. For example, the Convention on Biological Diversity specifically mentions the use of economic incentives. Article 11, on incentive measures, states that: "Each Contracting Party shall, as far as possible and as appropriate, adopt economically and socially sound measures that act as incentives for the conservation and sustainable use of components of biological diversity." The Kyoto Protocol also recognizes the potential for market-based instruments which allow both project-based offset trading (Articles 6 and 12) and emissions rights trading (Article 17).

Market-based instruments have several advantageous characteristics. They allow private decisionmakers greater flexibility (which helps reduce private costs); they generally are easier to implement than standards or other regulations; and they can reduce government costs, either by eliminating the need for subsidies or by raising revenues (taxes or fees). Market-based instruments have been used successfully in the United States at the national level to reduce sulfur emissions, and have been suggested for global use to reduce greenhouse gas emissions.

One type of market-based intervention is pricing resources appropriately to reflect the external social costs of resource use, including environmental damages resulting from emissions, release of effluents, or resource depletion. These prices are referred to as "full cost pricing." Often, the costs of damage to the environment are not accounted for in the unregulated marketplace—they are thus called externalities. Including environmental externalities

in the price signals shaped by government policies could affect individual and organizational behavior, leading to more environment-friendly outcomes (see box N for a description of related efforts to include stocks and flows of environmental resources in measures of national wealth, and hence provide information for more environmentally sound economic decisionmaking).

Another type of market mechanism is the trading of emission rights. Once governments set a cap on the amount of a substance that can be released into the environment, polluters can decide who among them will make the largest cutbacks. Other promising market-based interventions are described on the following pages. For example, if different firms have different marginal costs of abatement (the amount it costs each firm to reduce pollution by a fixed amount), it will be more efficient for the firms to trade pollution abatement requirements among themselves—each firm determining if it is cheaper to reduce its own pollution or pay another firm to expand its own pollution abatement activities to meet the obligations of *both* firms. In this way, the total target reduction in abatement can be met in the least expensive manner. The environment benefits as a result of reduced pollution, and the economy benefits from achieving this goal in the most economical manner.

Eliminating harmful subsidies

Subsidies often harm the environment. Many countries currently subsidize activities that lead to environmental degradation. For example, subsidies that reduce the prices of fossil fuels encourage their use and the accompanying emissions of greenhouse gases, and subsidies that keep water prices low for large-scale farms encourage over-irrigation and depletion of freshwater supplies. Subsidies for energy, roads, water, and agriculture in developing and

Box N

New approaches to resource accounting

Data and information are essential for incorporating the value of environmental goods and services into economic decisions. New approaches to using and presenting data on environmental assets are beginning to improve resource management. An example of this sort of approach is a set of new techniques that value stocks and flows of natural capital in economic terms and accounts. These new techniques try to address the inherent shortcomings of traditional measures of value by taking into account the values of renewable and non-renewable resources and adjusting standard economic measures to account for depletion of these re-

Wealth shares across selected regions, 1994

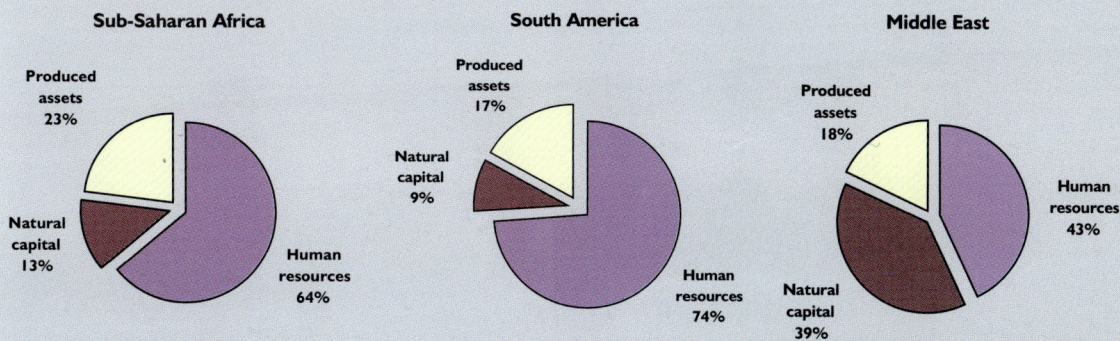

Sub-Saharan Africa

Produced assets 23%

Natural capital 13%

Human resources 64%

South America

Produced assets 17%

Natural capital 9%

Human resources 74%

Middle East

Produced assets 18%

Human resources 43%

Natural capital 39%

Note: Sub-Saharan Africa does not include data on Nigeria.
Source: World Bank. 1997. *Expanding the Measure of Wealth: Indicators of Environmentally Sustainable Development.* Washington, D.C.

sources. If, for example, national accounts can be modified to include an expanded *measure of national wealth*—including the value of stocks of living and non-living resources, human and social capital (combined as human resources), as well as manufactured capital—then changes in total wealth per capita (including the value of environmental goods and services) become a useful indicator of sustainability. Although the year-to-year values change slowly, trends over time indicate the sustainability of the system. A country's development can be considered sustainable if its total wealth per capita does not decrease over time. Another measure tracks year-to-year changes in the flow of savings and investments. This measure, called *"genuine savings"* starts with annual savings rates and makes adjustments for resource depletion and pollution. A positive genuine savings rate is a strong indication that the country is on a sustainable growth path.

Some preliminary attempts have been made by the World Bank to estimate both genuine savings and wealth per capita for several countries, by valuing stocks of manufactured assets, natural resources and human and social capital. These efforts have contributed to a growing realization that sustainable development will require maintenance, or even expansion, of at least four kinds of capital:

- Natural capital, or environmentally derived goods and services
- Financial or "human-made capital," such as machines, factories, buildings, and other infrastructure
- Human capital, including human capacity, as measured by educational and health status
- Social capital, including cultural and other social institutions that help provide a sense of identity and social cohesion.

Adequate human and social capital are necessary enabling conditions for successful governance, without which it is difficult to implement policy initiatives to promote the use of environmentally benign technologies and practices.

transition economies are estimated to total over $240 billion per year. One study of fossil fuel subsidies found that the amount of money paid by governments for energy subsidies worldwide is equivalent to paying $40 per ton of carbon released into the atmosphere!

The removal of subsidies that harm the environment can produce multiple benefits by reducing demand for previously subsidized resources and thus reducing pressure on the environment; freeing fiscal resources for other uses; and increasing economic efficiency by minimizing price distortions (see box O). An OECD study calculates that removing fossil fuel subsidies worldwide would reduce global emissions by 18 percent, compared with emissions projected for the year 2050, and could increase global real incomes by 0.7 percent annually (incomes in non-OECD countries would rise by 1.6 per cent). It is important to recognize, however, that the elimination of subsidies will be resisted by stakeholders whose income will be affected by the change.

Targeted subsidies

Not all subsidies are harmful. Sometimes subsidies are needed to promote improved technologies or practices and achieve environmental goals. One example is the use of government subsidies to make the development and production of substitutes for ozone-depleting substances (ODS) more affordable,

---

Box O

Subsidy reform in the coal sector in China

Since the mid-1980s, China has made remarkable progress in reducing energy subsidies, particularly in the coal sector, which produces more than 70 percent of the country's energy. Subsidy rates for coal have fallen from 61 percent in 1984 to 11 percent in 1995. The amount of money spent subsidizing fossil fuels (based on the difference between domestic and world prices) fell from an estimated $25 billion in 1990-91 to $10 billion in 1995-96. It also has been reported that the budgetary subsidy from China's central government to cover the operating losses in state-owned coal mines decreased from $750 million (1.1 percent of total government expenditures) in 1993 to $240 million (0.26 percent of government expenditures) in 1995. At the same time, China removed price controls on coal, and encouraged the development of non-state-owned coal mines.

Cooling tower of a thermal power plant.

Currently, these private mines produce about 50 percent of the country's coal. About 80 percent of coal is now sold at international prices.

Subsidy reform in China has produced multiple benefits: energy savings, financial savings, and reduced emissions of greenhouse gases. The economic performance of coal mines has improved rapidly: Estimated operating losses of state-owned mines dropped from $1.4 billion in 1990 to $230 million in 1994. These reform measures in the energy sector have reduced government spending and—along with the structural adjustment and technological change—have contributed to energy conservation and environmental protection. Energy intensity in China has fallen by about 30 percent since 1985, implying that energy consumption (in oil equivalents) and CO_2 emissions are now, respectively, 0.3 billion metric tons less and 1.1 billion metric tons less than would have been the case if the reform had not taken place.

thus enabling countries to meet the Montreal Protocol goals of phasing out ODS production and use. Other examples of targeted subsidies to encourage environmentally and socially desirable practices include state support for reforestation, and subsidies to reduce the prices of energy-efficient technologies, recycled products, alternative fuels, and sustainably-harvested wood and non-wood products.

Targeted subsidies are particularly critical for the success of alternative energy technologies. Before these technologies can enter the marketplace competitively, they must be researched and developed and may require subsidies to reduce their costs and encourage their adoption by the private sector.

While the use of targeted subsidies goes against the general trend of reducing government intervention in the marketplace, their use can sometimes be justified, particularly if offered on a temporary basis to encourage the use of new approaches or technologies during market introduction or development. In Indonesia, for example, the government subsidized the use of new, alternative pest-control methods to encourage farmers to use environmentally friendly methods of rice farming, and to use chemical sprays only as a last resort. Within three years farmers were using 90 percent less pesticide, rice yields were increasing, and a number of environmental benefits (such as water quality improvements and protection of local biodiversity) were realized.

Taxes and pollution charges

Just as targeted subsidies can encourage certain practices, taxes and pollution charges can be used to discourage certain behaviors. Even if the market price of a product reflects its full cost of production, other external costs to the environment or human health may not be reflected in the price. Environ-

The removal of pesticide subsidies results in more careful pesticide application and reduced environmental damage.

mental taxes on such products can help raise prices to more accurately reflect these additional costs to society and the environment. These types of measures have three main benefits: They can act as an incentive to reduce pollution (pollution charges), use resources more efficiently (taxes on environmental resources), and generate revenues. Sulfur and carbon taxes have been used in different regions to discourage the use of certain polluting fuels, thereby reducing emissions of these substances, while also raising government revenues.

In contrast to quotas or emission standards, pollution charges do not set limits on emissions or production. Instead, firms or other regulated entities are free to either emit pollutants and pay the tax, or pay for installation of controls to reduce emissions. The challenge for government regulators is to calculate the level of charge or tax that will change behavior sufficiently to achieve environmental objectives. Taxes and charges have been placed on outputs—industrial emissions and discharges of pollutants to waterways—as well as inputs to production such as energy, water, fertilizers, and pesticides. Taxes on the sale of goods also can re-

65

lic involvement can help focus government attention on environmental management.

Product information, eco-labeling, and information disclosure

Information on the environmental impacts of producing specific products can assist consumers in making informed decisions about the purchase of goods and services. For example, product labeling and rating can provide important information on energy usage, which consumers can use as a criterion for buying such goods as home appliances and automobiles. Provision of such product information and labeling requires effective standards and rating systems, which can be developed in conjunction with trade or professional associations and other stakeholders (see box R). Other types of information disclosure from energy providers also can encourage savings. Utility bills can be structured to convey information about usage patterns, comparisons of one's usage with that of other consumers and with monthly usage in previous years, and potential resource savings that may be achieved through changes in these patterns. Municipalities can also encourage recycling and water conservation through public information campaigns.

Voluntary agreements

Voluntary agreements can be very effective tools for improving environmental performance, when participants are informed and motivated to make changes. Examples of such agreements include voluntary programs to reduce pollutant emissions, reduce energy consumption, conserve natural resources, and increase recycling.

Corporations may have a number of motivations for participating in voluntary agreements, such as reducing the risk that performance standards will be imposed by government regulation, achieving

Box R

The EcoWatch Project in the Philippines

In 1996 Philippine President Ramos signed a memorandum of agreement with 23 industry associations (representing about 2,000 companies) to formally launch an eco-labeling campaign called the Industrial EcoWatch Project. The project is designed to provide a strong incentive for industries to comply with environmental regulations, and to reward industries whose environmental performance exceeds standard requirements. As part of the project, the government has set up a five-level grading system to categorize the environmental performance of these firms. The inclusion of industry representatives in the creation of this system was critical to its success, because the private firms—by signing the EcoWatch project agreement—have committed themselves to supporting its implementation. The first stages of the project—setting broad guidelines for the five categories, identifying 259 priority wastewater dischargers, and rating performance in about 100 of them—are underway, and the program is to be expanded.

favorable public relations, and reducing costs by reducing energy wastage and loss of valuable products in the form of waste discharges. Examples of voluntary agreements in the United States and Europe include negotiated targets for achieving emissions reductions, voluntary adoption of high-efficiency products or processes, cooperative research and development, and agreements to monitor and report emissions.

Another type of voluntary activity involves the adoption of energy-efficiency standards for residential and commercial buildings. In such cases manufacturers and builders agree—without government-mandated legislation—to produce building components or construct buildings that meet defined energy-use criteria. The resulting reductions in energy consumption yield a wide range of environmental benefits, including reduced emissions of pollutants that cause smog, acid rain, deposition of heavy metals, and climate change.

The success of voluntary agreements can be greatly enhanced by a combination of factors: the threat of government regulation if environmentally harmful practices continue, the availability of accurate information on the costs and benefits of implementing changes, and the capability to monitor results.

RESEARCH, DEVELOPMENT, AND DEMONSTRATION

Providing an improved standard of living for a growing global population without compromising environmental systems requires development of new technologies and processes that use energy and materials in an efficient manner. Research, development, and demonstration (RD&D) efforts involving governments, universities, and the private sector are critical to ensuring the development of new products, energy sources, and techniques that will increase production of needed goods and services with reduced environmental impacts.

RD&D is important not only for the development of new technologies, but also to help overcome barriers that may be limiting the application of existing technologies by improving their performance, reliability, and market penetration. The "demonstration" component of RD&D is critical for providing information on actual performance, installation costs, training needs, maintenance requirements, and other aspects of technology application in market settings.

While the private sector must play a major role in RD&D, there is a strong rationale for governmental support because of the high costs of much RD&D and the need to protect the intellectual property of private firms, ensuring that they receive the benefits associated with their investments in new technologies. Unfortunately, public sector investment in fields important for environmental protection is declining. For example, energy research and development in OECD countries has decreased 50 percent in real terms over the past 10 years and, of the remaining funds, less than 20 percent is spent on improving energy efficiency or on renewable energies; 80 percent or more is still spent on developing fossil and nuclear energy. Much potential exists to achieve environmental goals by renewing government commitments to support RD&D in the energy field.

IMPROVING NATIONAL AND INTERNATIONAL POLICY COORDINATION

International conventions and statements provide a set of goals for meeting human needs in an environmentally sustainable fashion. Unfortunately, the single-issue focus of these conventions encourages the implementation of measures that may fulfill one environmental objective at the expense of others. This creates the potential for unproductive competition among environmental and developmental goals and encourages strategies that may be beneficial to one sector (such as increasing food production through the increased use of irrigation) but result in harm to others (non-sustainable use of water resources, salinization of soils). Potential measures to overcome this problem include coordinating environmental policy formulation among sectoral authorities at the national level, and improving coordination of environmental and sustainable development initiatives among intergovernmental organizations—including efforts under the international environmental conventions.

National Policy Coordination

Government institutions usually are structured to meet narrow mandates; to provide food, water, or electricity. In many cases responsibility for safeguarding the environment is separated from that of meeting these basic needs. Too often there is little recognition of how sectoral policies interact, contribute to local environmental problems, or accelerate global change. Addressing global environmental problems will require creative thinking about how to design governmental institutions to minimize tradeoffs and improve coordination at all levels and between all sectors. Even national-level government institutions with a broad mandate to develop national policy to address global environmental issues generally disconnect responsibilities for specific environmental issues. This compartmentalization is reinforced by the structure of national-level participation in the international conventions: each convention generally has its own constituency within each country, and each country creates separate decisionmaking bodies and national delegations for each of the conventions. Scarce resources within each government are dissipated by this separation of convention-related activities, and opportunities to identify potential areas of common interest and synergies are missed. For example, several of the conventions call for the sustainable management/use of land and water resources, with varying goals (such as enhancing GHG sinks and reservoirs, protecting biological diversity, safeguarding aquatic ecosystems, managing forests to meet human needs, halting land degradation). Coordinating efforts to achieve these convention-specific goals within countries would enable national implementing agencies to cooperate in regional initiatives or in their choice of measures, leading to more effective protection of resources.

Some specific measures for national policy integration include:

- Integration of national procedures to negotiate and implement the various conventions
- Integration of national data collection and reporting for the various conventions to which a country is a Party
- Encouragement of research and monitoring activities that can meet the needs of more than one convention and increase understanding of the linkages among the underlying scientific issues.

International Policy Coordination

Effective international coordination is another critical need for implementing cost-effective solutions to linked global environmental problems. Unfortunately, coordination and cooperation often are lacking at the international level, in part because the existing international organizations and mechanisms have a single-issue focus analogous to the sectoral organization of national governments. The

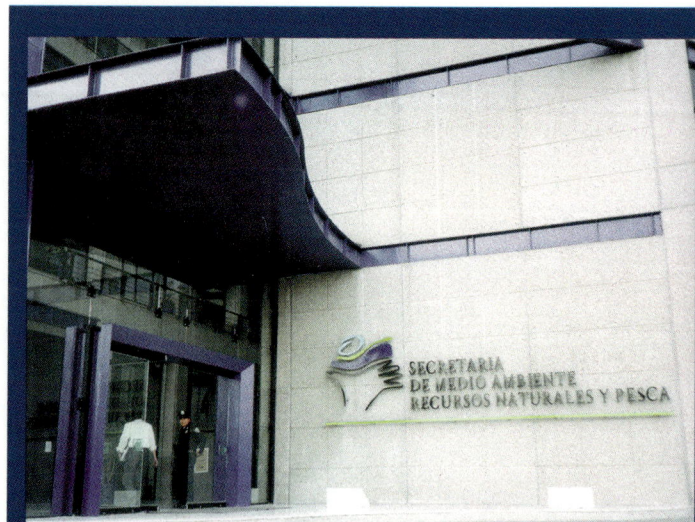

Mexico has established a special ministry to manage the environment, natural resources, and fisheries.

growing need for coherence among intergovernmental organizations that address environmental issues and/or sustainable development was highlighted by the UN General Assembly Special Session in June 1997.

The convention secretariats are exploring potential mechanisms to improve coordination among convention-related activities. Specific options to be considered include:

- Integration of national reporting requirements. Many of the conventions call for Parties to file and periodically update national reports and action plans. Combining these reporting requirements would allow the reports to more carefully examine the linkages among the issues from a national perspective.

- Design of training and capacity-building programs that cover several conventions, for example, collaboration among the Secretariats of the Biodiversity, Desertification, and Climate Change Conventions to provide assistance to governments on capacity-building activities

- Integration of critical mechanisms and processes, for example, improved coordination of activities under the Global Environment Facility (GEF), the financial mechanism of several of the conventions.

- Integrated scientific assessments. The convention bodies could cooperate in producing assessments that examine the linkages among the ecological processes addressed by the different conventions.

- Cooperation in producing outreach materials to inform the public about the relationships among environmental issues.

- The potential for integrating meetings of the convention bodies—in both place and time—should be explored, to minimize the time that minis-

ters and other national officials spend participating in intergovernmental meetings.

In addition to these specific suggestions, some far-sighted observers have envisioned an over-arching legal instrument or forum that would review and verify attainment of global environmental goals in an integrated manner.

Improved national and international coordination can expand awareness of the linkages among global environmental issues and promote the development of integrated approaches to address these issues and sustainably meet human needs.

THE LESSONS OF EFFECTIVE POLICYMAKING AND IMPLEMENTATION

Solving environmental problems and switching to more sustainable development strategies will involve tradeoffs. Practical solutions often require balancing competing needs; it is important to make well-informed choices that capture as many benefits as possible, without delaying action to wait for "perfect" solutions. The previous discussion of policy instruments illustrates a number of ways in which environmental goals can be advanced. Although environmental policies traditionally have focused on a single issue, now the challenge is to identify policies that can simultaneously produce benefits in meeting several environmental goals.

Four lessons can be drawn from this review of environmental policies: the importance of ensuring administrative sustainability; securing financial sustainability; the benefits of building constituencies for change; and the need to achieve policy integration.

Ensuring administrative sustainability

Since the environment is a relatively new concern at the level of national governments, few countries

71

have well-established bureaucracies for environmental management. As a result, this management function commonly is housed in a new, often weak, ministry or agency. Technically trained staff, laboratory facilities, and other support often are inadequate or nonexistent. It is thus important to develop policies that do not require elaborate and expensive administrative support.

In many cases the new policies can be implemented by other, sectoral ministries as environmental concerns are "mainstreamed" into ongoing activities. This approach is facilitated by the growing awareness of the interlinkages among environmental systems. The policies reviewed in this report highlight a number of innovative approaches to improved management, sometimes involving policies that are self-policing or make minimal new administrative demands.

Achieving financial sustainability

The widespread trend to reduce government spending means that little additional public funding may be available to address national and global environmental concerns in the near term. This underscores the importance of policy initiatives that generate financial resources, for example, by removing environmentally damaging subsidies (such as those for fossil-based energy or fertilizer), imposing environmental taxes that help account for externalities (such as damage from air and water pollution), or charging users a fair price for the benefits that they receive from the environment.

For environmental issues of worldwide importance, international funding mechanisms such as the GEF and the multilateral fund created under the Montreal Protocol offer limited financial support to developing countries. The GEF, since its inception in 1991, has provided US$2.0 billion (by June 1998)

to address biodiversity loss, stratospheric ozone depletion, global warming, and the management of international waters. Although this sum clearly is not sufficient to solve these global problems, GEF resources have provided significant leverage to make a useful start, especially in the fields of ozone depletion and biodiversity, and have been useful in promoting new technologies to mitigate global climate change.

The declining trend in government spending highlights the growing importance of the private sector as a potential ally in the shift to sustainability.

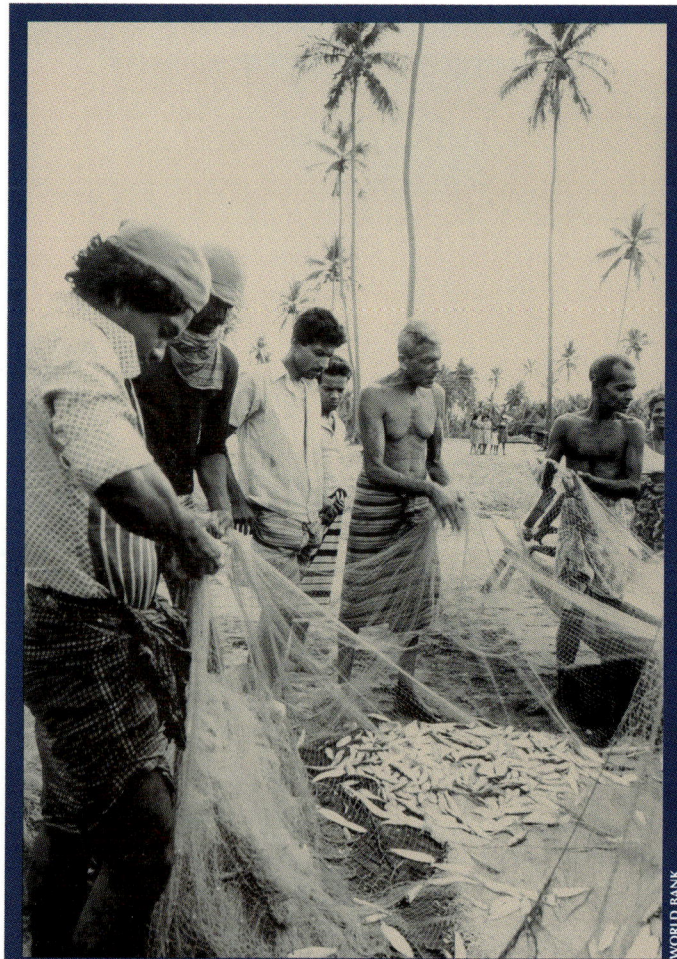

Traditional fishermen often rely on community resource management to maintain production.

Not only is the private sector by far the largest source of investment funds, but, in a number of cases, private firms can be relatively easily encouraged to implement policies that produce multiple economic and environmental benefits. As noted earlier, the private sector provides nearly US$260 billion per year in investments and loans in developing countries, in comparison with US$50 billion per year in loans from the development banks and less than US$1 billion per year from the GEF. However, since approximately 90 percent of private funding has been flowing to only 12 countries undergoing fast-paced economic development, private sector funds alone are not sufficient to address the global problems. This increases the importance of efficiently using the financing that is available from governments' domestic budgets, overseas development assistance, and multilateral development funds.

Funding for environmental policy implementation could be more efficiently managed if public and private lenders—who currently have different priorities, lending criteria, and reporting requirements—established common lending policies favoring projects with multiple environmental and social benefits. The establishment of such common criteria, although difficult, would facilitate cooperation among different national ministries in the preparation of proposals that take advantage of the linkages among the issues.

Building constituencies for change

Whenever policy change involves controlling "rights" or reducing economic gains, however, there will be resistance from those whose financial interests are negatively affected in the short term. In addition to efforts to educate these interests about the environmental necessity for such changes, political will is necessary to implement effective change

that can overcome vested interests. This is particularly true for environmental policy changes, since many of the gains from resource extraction accrue to a few powerful companies, whereas the benefits of environmental protection are dispersed among a broad base of people.

Environmental progress often is made when an informed public demands environmental protection from its elected officials, or successfully puts pressure on companies to change their practices through publicity campaigns and product boycotts. Environmental improvements, in turn, may require some sacrifices by individuals, such as lower personal consumption of resource-intensive and polluting goods and services. In order to protect the global environment, people and their governments must be willing to make changes for the common good.

Achieving policy integration

Over the past two decades, the world has made great progress in identifying environmental challenges, and many governments, industries, and expert groups have made a promising start in developing policies, technologies, and programs that can lead to more sustainable forms of development. Most of these successes have been at the local or national level, within the jurisdiction of municipal, state and provincial, and national governments. Small groups of nations also have dealt successfully with common transboundary issues, such as air pollution, water rights, and the protection of migratory species.

However, continued global environmental degradation indicates that coordinated international action is required to improve the global stewardship of environmental resources

The policymaking challenge is to consider various options to meet pressing economic, social, and environmental needs; recognize the links among issues; and choose those policies that offer the greatest chance of producing multiple benefits—both to the nation and the global community—without imposing excessive costs on nations. This will entail designing and implementing policies that address environmental problems in a cost-effective manner and that can be implemented in a world of weak institutions, lack of political will, limited human and financial resources, and vested interests. The policies also must move beyond the prevailing single-issue view of environmental problems to achieve integrated approaches to implementation and build on the synergies and links among environmental systems.

Part V

The Importance of Timing

GIVEN THE EMERGING PIC-ture of the serious risks posed by global environmental changes, decisionmakers must decide how to steer current development patterns in more sustainable directions, and how to do so quickly. Although we are gaining increasing scientific understanding of the potential consequences of human-induced changes to the global environment, it is difficult to forecast the timing, location, and detailed cost implications of many of the changes. It is important, however, to consider these uncertainties in the context of information indicating that most changes to the global environment cannot be reversed quickly, if at all, due to the long time-scales associated with the underlying chemical, physical, and ecological processes.

The implications of these time-scales are apparent in the case of stratospheric ozone depletion. Despite the implemen-

tation of an international agreement to eliminate emissions of ozone-depleting substances, the ozone layer will not recover until the middle of the twenty-first century. Even longer time-scales may apply to the issue of climate change: If emissions of greenhouse gases cause large-scale environmental impacts, as projected by the Intergovernmental Panel on Climate Change, the time needed to recover from damages would be centuries to millennia, even if greenhouse gas emissions were to cease. In the case of biological diversity, restoration or rehabilitation of degraded ecosystems would take decades to centuries, and for some ecosystems might not be possible, while species extinction is irreversible.

There also is a risk that major environmental changes may not be uniform or predictable over long timeframes. Environmental systems can undergo non-linear

Box S

Time dimensions of human and natural systems

Environmental systems

The life cycles of physical, chemical, and ecosystem processes can vary widely. The atmospheric residence time for many greenhouse and ozone-depleting gases exceeds a century. The equilibration of sea level to a given atmospheric concentration of greenhouse gases takes centuries to millennia. Soil carbon persists for more than a century, while most soils store water for less than a month. Ecosystem rehabilitation may take decades or longer, and species extinction is irreversible. In addition, some natural systems have non-linear responses after certain thresholds, and rapidly switch to new and unpredictable states.

Projected rise in sea level

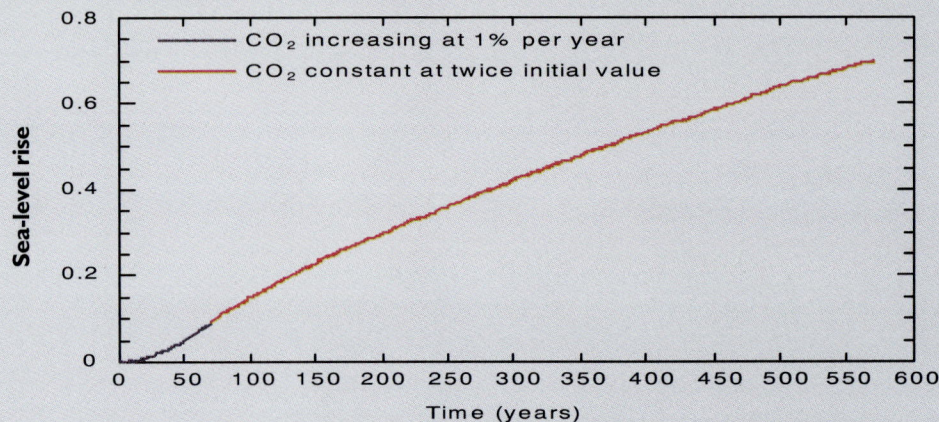

The rise in sea level due to thermal expansion alone (which accounts for about half of the total rise over the next decades), following an increase in atmospheric concentrations of CO_2 of 1% per year for 70 years (blue), and climate stabilization for a further 500 years (red).

Source: R. Nicholls, Middlesex University in the U.K. Meteorological Office. 1997. *Climate Change and Its Impact: A Global Perspective.* Brittanic Crown Copyright.

Capital stock turnover

Without premature retirement, the turnover time for capital stock ranges from years to decades. Residential buildings are used for many decades, even centuries, while power plants and other industrial structures remain useful for 50 years or more. Household goods such as refrigerators, stoves, and washers and dryers commonly last 20 years or more, and automobiles and many consumer goods may last more than a decade.

Diffusion of new technologies

Technological diffusion—from the point of innovation to full implementation in the marketplace—typically takes several decades. During the European industrial revolution, it took about 50 years for coal to replace the then-predominant energy source: fuelwood. During the current century, it took a similar amount of time for oil and gas to replace coal as the dominant global fossil fuel. The widespread adoption of a new generation of automobiles would likely take more than 20 years, while the transition from a fossil fuel economy to a predominantly carbon-free energy economy is likely to take half a century or more—long enough to allow for the replacement of most technological systems and infrastructures without a premature decommissioning of capital.

Social change

It takes about one human lifetime to halt population growth after a population has achieved replacement fertility (about 2.1 children per woman). Social and production patterns change even more slowly. Patterns of desired fertility, levels and types of consumption, and means of generating that consumption have evolved over centuries, if not millennia.

changes, rapidly shifting from one state to another. Studies of ancient sediments reveal that large changes in the global climate system can occur very rapidly—over periods as short as decades. A recent example was the non-linear response of the ozone layer over Antarctica to small additions of chlorine above a threshold level of two parts per billion. The incremental increase in the level of this ozone-depleting chemical caused a large decline in ozone levels when the threshold was reached.

Furthermore, rapidly increasing demands for energy and biological resources—and the environmental degradation associated with meeting these demands—reduce the buffering capacity of the environment, leaving societies more vulnerable to natural climatic fluctuations such as droughts.

The speed with which human society can shift production cycles in order to respond to environmental change is limited, due to the long time-scales and large investments needed for the turnover of capital stock and the introduction of new technologies into the marketplace. The natural inertia of human and policy systems further retards our ability to respond rapidly to changes.

Decisionmakers have to weigh the pros and cons of action versus delay. Some people argue that delaying responses to global environmental problems can reduce the overall costs of action, because more cost-effective technologies may be developed in the future to address certain problems. However, a delay strategy can allow the rate and eventual magnitude of environmental changes to increase, magnifying the eventual costs of adapting to adverse impacts on human health, ecological systems, and socioeconomic sectors.

Decisionmakers therefore must decide to what degree they want to take precautionary measures. As discussed throughout this report, some options

for adapting to or mitigating the potential effects of global environmental changes can be justified for other reasons, such as the abatement of local and regional air and water pollution. Recognition of these types of multiple benefits from carefully chosen actions can help decisionmakers select measures that yield a wide range of benefits and receive public and political support.

The challenge is to identify—in spite of scientific uncertainties—prudent, cost-effective, and adaptive management approaches that can be implemented now and will contribute to a more sustainable future. Because significant scientific uncertainties still exist in our understanding of global warming and sea-level rise, for example, a nation may be reluctant to relocate existing coastal infrastructure at significant present cost to avoid less certain future damages. However, siting new infrastructure to avoid exposure to a future sea-level rise will not likely add to current costs and will yield a significant payback if sea levels do rise. While societies may not be able to afford to quickly retrofit current equipment or change practices to respond fully to emerging environmental concerns, they can begin to make investments and decisions that will advance their future ability to meet these challenges.

While there is a natural desire to eliminate uncertainty before taking action, such an inclination must be tempered by the long timeframes associated with both human and natural systems. If nations wait to respond to problems that are developing today, future generations will inherit a less sustainable, more degraded Earth. The inertia of both human and natural systems should spur nations to take a precautionary approach in addressing the interlinked global environmental problems and act today to allow the future achievement of sustainable development goals.

In order to protect the environment, the precautionary approach shall be widely applied by States according to their capabilities. Where there are threats of serious or irreversible damage, lack of full scientific certainty shall not be used as a reason for postponing cost-effective measures to prevent environmental degradation.

— From the 1992 Rio Declaration on Environment and Development,
a statement of principles defining the rights and responsibilities
of nations as they pursue human development and well-being.

The Major Challenges for Development

Reducing poverty

- 1.3 billion people live on less than US$1 per day; 3 billion people live on less than US$2 per day.
- 1.3 billion people live without clean water, 2 billion without sanitation, and 2 billion without electricity.
- The global development path is diverging, and the gap between the rich and the poor increasing.
- Increase literacy among all groups of people. About 130 million children are not enrolled in primary schools (103 million of these are girls).

Doubling available food without excessive use of synthetic chemicals, conversion of natural habitats, or degradation of marginal lands

- Today 800 million people are malnourished.
- 25 billion tons of topsoil are lost annually.
- 1.5–2.5 million hectares of irrigated land have been lost to agricultural production due to salinization.
- Close to three-quarters of oceanic fish stocks are depleted, declining, or fully exploited.
- Available food will need to double in the next 35 years because of population and economic growth.
- The last doubling of world food production occurred over 25 years, primarily using irrigation, chemical inputs, high yielding seeds, and intensive fishing techniques. The next doubling is expected to be more difficult, and may require an expansion of land used for agriculture, including forested and marginal lands, as well as more intensive aquaculture.

Providing energy services without environmental degradation

- Many countries are promoting fossil fuel energy policies and practices that are environmentally unsustainable and cause environmental degradation at the local (particulates and smog), regional (acid deposition) and global (climate change) scales.
- The 2 billion people without access to electricity usually cook using traditional fuels with poor ventilation, leading to a high incidence of respiratory infections, diseases, and deaths in women and children.
- Today, 1.4 billion people are exposed to dangerous levels of outdoor air pollution leading to millions of premature deaths.
- Energy use is projected to double within 30 years, in large part due to economic growth in developing countries.

Providing access to water to meet basic needs

- One-third of the world's population lives in water-stressed areas where lack of water is the major reason for slow economic development.
- In 2025 it is projected that two-thirds of the world's population will live in water stressed areas.
- Poor water and sanitation contribute to infant mortality and low life expectancy.

Developing healthy urban environments

- In 1960 less than 25 percent of the developing world's population lived in cities. This figure is projected to increase to over 50 percent by 2005 and 66 percent by 2025.
- By 2015 there will be 33 megacities with populations of 8 million people, and 500 cities with populations of 1 million people.
- Within 25 years the number of urban poor is estimated to reach 1 billion, more than double today.
- In developing countries 220 million urban residents lack access to potable drinking water, 350 million have no access to basic sanitation, and 1 billion have no solid waste collection service.
- Air pollution, primarily particulates and lead, is a serious problem in more than half of the world's 20 major cities, leading to significant numbers of premature deaths and economic losses.

A Synopsis of Eight Major Global Environmental Issues

Global Climate Change

Current trend

- The Earth's global mean surface temperature has warmed by about half a degree Centigrade over the last 100 years.
- The six warmest years this century have occurred since 1990, and eight of the next ten warmest have occurred since 1980.
- The amount and spatial and temporal patterns of precipitation are changing.
- Average sea level has increased by 15-25 centimeters during the last 100 years.
- Glaciers are retreating worldwide.

Underlying causes of change

- Human activities, primarily energy-use and land-use practices, are increasing the atmospheric concentrations of greenhouse gases and, in some regions, aerosols.
- Greenhouse gases warm the atmosphere, while aerosols tend to cool the atmosphere.
- The balance of scientific evidence suggests a discernible human influence on the Earth's climate.

Projected impact of human activities on the climate system

- Without globally coordinated policies to specifically address human-induced climate change, the concentrations of greenhouse gases in the atmosphere are projected to increase significantly. The atmospheric concentration of carbon dioxide is projected to increase from 360 parts per million by volume (ppmv) today to between 500 and 900 ppmv in 2100, depending on population and economic growth rates, energy prices, and the development and deployment of new technologies.
- Global mean surface temperatures are projected to increase by between 1.0 and 3.5 degrees Centigrade by 2100, a rate faster than anything observed during the last 10,000 years.
- Sea levels are projected to rise by 15-95 centimeters by 2100.
- Global warming caused by increases in the atmospheric concentrations of greenhouse gases can only be reversed very slowly because of the century-scale atmospheric residence times of the gases and the large thermal inertia of the oceans.

Social and economic consequences of projected changes

- Projected changes in climate may result in: adverse effects on human health, in particular an increase in heat-stress mortality and vector-borne diseases, with potentially tens of millions of additional cases of malaria per year; changes in the boundaries, structure, and functioning of ecological systems, especially forests where there could be a near-term die back and a shift in boundaries of between 150 and 650 kilometers polewards; a decrease in agricultural production in the tropics and subtropics, even if total global food production does not drop; less predictable availability of freshwater; and the displacement of tens of millions of people from small island states and low lying deltaic areas, if sea levels increase by one meter
- Developing countries will be particularly vulnerable to the impacts of climate change because of their limited institutional and financial capabilities.
- The cost of damage associated with a climate change caused by a doubling of atmospheric carbon dioxide has been estimated to lie between 1.5 and 2.0 percent of world GDP, with damages in developing countries in the range of 2-9 percent of GDP.

Technologies, policies, and measures to mitigate the projected changes in climate

- A range of cost-effective technologies and policies can be used now in both developed and developing countries to markedly reduce the emissions of greenhouse gases from the energy supply (more efficient production; fuel switching, e.g., coal to gas; nuclear power; renewable energies, e.g., solar, wind, modern biomass, hydroelectric; and carbon sequestration) and energy demand sectors (more efficient buildings, transportation, and industry sectors), as well as changes in land management, including forestry and agricultural practices.
- Policy measures to accelerate technology development, diffusion, and transfer are available, but need wider application if emissions reductions are to be achieved.
- By the year 2100, the world's commercial energy system will be replaced at least twice, providing opportunities to use new, better-performing technologies over coming years without the premature retirement of capital stock.

Status of international agreements

- The Framework Convention on Climate Change (FCCC) was signed at the 1992 Earth Summit in Rio, and has since been ratified by 164 countries. The aim of Annex I countries (OECD and the FSU) was to limit their emissions of greenhouse gases to their 1990 level in the year 2000.
- In December 1997 industrialized countries agreed to reduce their emissions of greenhouse gases by an average of 5.2 percent during the period 2008-2012 relative to 1990 (Kyoto Protocol).

Loss of Biological Diversity

Current trend
- Human activities are directly responsible for creating agroecosystems and cultural landscapes at the expense of impoverishment of many natural communities and the reduction in ecosystem services.
- Since 1600, 484 animals and 654 plant species are recorded as having gone extinct, although this is almost certainly an underestimate. Assuming animals and plants have an average lifespan of 5 to 10 million years, the current extinction rate for these species has been conservatively estimated to be 50 to 100 times the average expected natural rate.

Underlying causes of change
- The primary causes underlying the loss of biodiversity include: (i) increasing demands for biological resources due to increasing populations and economic development; (ii) inappropriate use of technologies; (iii) failure of markets to recognize the true value of biodiversity; (iv) failure of economic markets to appropriate the global value of biodiversity at the local level; (v) institutional failures to regulate the use of biological resources; (vi) human migration, travel, and international trade; and (vii) failure of people to consider the long-term consequences of their actions.
- These underlying causes manifest themselves through the loss, fragmentation, and conversion of natural habitats; overexploitation of wild resources; introduction of exotic species; air and water pollution; and more recently, long-term climate change.

Projected impact of human activities on biodiversity
- For some groups of vertebrates and plants, between 5 and 20 percent of the identified species are already listed as being threatened with extinction in the foreseeable future.
- Assuming that recent rates of loss of closed tropical forests continue (0.5-1 percent globally per year) for the next 30 years, the equilibrium number of species would be reduced by 5-10 percent. This would be equivalent to 1,000 to 10,000 times faster than the expected natural rate of species extinction.
- Even if species do not become extinct, habitat loss and fragmentation will put many of them into severe decline, including the loss of distinct populations and the severe loss of genetic diversity that keeps any species healthy.

Social and economic consequences of projected changes
- Loss of biological resources and biodiversity interferes with essential ecological functions such as regulation of water run-off, the control of soil erosion, the assimilation of wastes and purification of water, and the cycling of carbon and other nutrients.
- In turn, this threatens food supplies, sources of wood, medicines and energy, recreation, and tourism.
- Loss of genetic diversity will affect the ability of ecological communities to resist or recover from disturbances and environmental change, including long-term climatic change.

Technologies, policies, and measures to reduce the loss of biodiversity
- The conservation and sustainable use of biodiversity needs to become an integral component of sectoral economic development (e.g., agriculture, forestry, coastal zone management) which would require correcting policy and market failures.
- A wide variety of in-situ (e.g., legal protection of endangered species and the establishment of protected areas and safe corridors), and ex-situ (arboreta, aquaria, botanical gardens, seed banks, gene banks, zoological gardens) techniques can be employed to conserve biodiversity.
- The equitable sharing of benefits from the use of biodiversity requires that the local, regional, and global benefits of biodiversity are appropriated at the local level through the creation of functioning markets.

Status of international agreements
- The Convention on Biological Diversity was signed in Rio and has since been ratified by 169 countries. In general, each country has the obligation to conserve and sustainably use its own biological diversity. However, mechanisms to promote this goal have only been developed to a limited extent.

Stratospheric Ozone Depletion

Current trend

- Stratospheric ozone has decreased since 1979 by about 5.4 percent at northern mid-latitudes in winter and spring; about 2.8 percent at northern mid-latitudes in summer and fall; and about 5.0 percent at southern mid-latitudes on a year-round basis. There is no discernible trend in the tropics and sub-tropics.
- Every springtime in Antarctica (fall in the northern hemisphere) more than 60 percent of stratospheric ozone is destroyed for a period of several months, creating what is commonly known as the hole in the ozone layer.
- Stratospheric ozone levels in the Arctic region have been unusually low in six of the last nine years in late winter and spring, with typically a 15 percent depletion.

Underlying causes of change

- Human activities have caused a six-fold increase in the abundance of stratospheric chlorine, and a smaller increase in stratospheric bromine. These increases have been caused through the production and emission of chlorofluorocarbons (used as aerosol propellants, solvents, air-conditioning fluids, and refrigerants), halons (used as fire retardants), and methyl chloroform and carbon tetrachloride (used as solvents).
- The annual springtime "Antarctic ozone hole" is caused by anthropogenic chlorine- and bromine-containing chemicals.
- The weight of scientific evidence suggests that the observed mid-latitude loss of ozone is, in large part, due to anthropogenic chlorine- and bromine-containing chemicals.

Projected impact of human activities on the ozone layer

- Stratospheric ozone depletion is projected to peak within the next several years because of the effectiveness of the Montreal Protocol and subsequent amendments and adjustments. The expected depletion is about 6 percent at northern mid-latitudes in winter and spring, about 3 percent at northern mid-latitudes in summer and fall, and about 5 percent at southern mid-latitudes on a year-round basis. These changes would be accompanied by increases in ground-level ultraviolet radiation of 7 percent, 4 percent, and 6 percent, respectively.
- Assuming full compliance with the Montreal Protocol and subsequent amendments and adjustments, the ozone layer in Antarctica and at mid-latitudes should fully recover by the middle of the next century. Thus important progress has been made in this area.

Social and economic consequences of projected changes

- Stratospheric ozone depletion leads to an increase in ground-level ultraviolet radiation, which can cause adverse consequences for human health (melanoma and non-melanoma skin cancer, eye cataracts and possible suppression of the human immune system), ecological systems (loss of productivity in terrestrial and aquatic ecosystems), air quality (increase in oxidant levels), and accelerated degradation of materials.

Technologies, policies, and measures to mitigate the projected changes

- Long-lived chlorofluorocarbons are being replaced by shorter lived halocarbons, which are environmentally more benign or by non-halogen-containing chemicals. The substitutes include, hydrochlorofluorocarbons (HCFCs), hydrofluorocarbons (HFCs), and perfluorocarbons (PFCs).
- However, even these shorter-lived chemicals are only transitional substitutes because the HCFCs still lead to ozone destruction, and all of them contribute to global warming.

Status of international agreements

- The Vienna Convention for the Protection of the Ozone Layer was signed in 1985, the Montreal Protocol on Substances that Deplete the Ozone Layer was signed in 1987 and was amended and adjusted in London in 1991, Copenhagen in 1993, and Vienna in 1996.
- The production and consumption of all chlorofluorocarbons, carbon tetrachloride, methyl chloroform, and halons has been banned in developed countries as of January 1996, and is to be banned by the year 2010 in developing countries.
- Control measures for other halocarbons, such as methyl bromide and the HCFCs, have also been negotiated.

Freshwater Degradation

Current trends
- There is an emerging 'water crisis' in some regions of the world. Today about one-third of the world's population is living under moderate or severe water stress, most notably in the Middle East and North Africa.
- 1.3 billion people lack access to adequate supply of safe water and 2 billion people do not have access to adequate sanitation. Water pollution is continuing to cause millions of preventable deaths every year, especially among children.
- 70 percent of the water withdrawn is used for irrigation; one-half is lost to seepage and evaporation.
- Hydrological and ecological functions of over one-half of all wetlands have been altered due to encroachment.
- Global freshwater biodiversity is declining significantly.
- Increasing water pollution affects water availability by imposing additional costs for treatment.
- Poor land use is imposing a heavy economic and environmental cost on water resources.

Underlying causes
- Population growth, income growth, and rapid urbanization are increasing water demands for municipal, industrial, agricultural, and hydroelectric generation.
- Water is treated as a social good and not an economic good, leading to its inefficient use, as in wasteful irrigation practices.
- Excessive reliance on government for water and wastewater services.
- Inadequate recognition of the health and environmental concerns associated with current practices.
- Uncoordinated management of water between sectors, institutions and nations, with little regard for conflicts or complementarities between social, economic and environmental objectives.
- Population pressures are increasing land degradation due to poor land management, thus worsening soil erosion and sediment transport in downstream areas.
- Growing water scarcity worsens the effects of natural droughts that are endemic in many parts of the world.

Projected impacts of human activities on fresh and marine water resources
- In 2025, up to two-thirds of the world's population, depending upon the rate of population growth, may experience moderate or severe water stress. These will mainly be people living in developing countries, whose limited technical, financial, and management capabilities will pose a disproportionate burden on their national economies.
- Water pollution will continue to degrade freshwater and marine ecosystems.
- Poor land use will continue to increase the frequency of flash floods, and will pollute coastal and marine ecosystems.

Social and economic consequences of projected changes
- Surface and groundwater quality will be further degraded.
- Provision of safe water in urban and rural areas will remain a major challenge in the future.
- Human health risks from inadequate sanitation will continue to be a major concern, especially in urban areas.
- Water use will need to be managed in a more holistic and multisectoral manner, i.e., agriculture, domestic, and industrial uses.
- Economic impacts of land degradation on water resources will be exacerbated.
- Conflicts between sectoral uses in some nations, and between nations in some regions of the world, will worsen. Tensions between riparian states sharing transboundary waters are likely to intensify.

Technologies, policies, and measures to mitigate the projected changes

At the national level, priorities include:
- Placing greater emphasis on integrated, cross-sectoral water resources management, addressing quantity and quality concerns jointly.
- Using river and groundwater basins as management units and recognizing freshwater, coastal, and marine environments as a management continuum.
- Recognizing water as a scarce economic good, and promoting cost-effective interventions.
- Supporting innovative and participatory efforts to manage water resources, and strengthening national capacities, including for women.
- Linking land-use management with sustainable, integrated water-resources management.
- Stimulate the adoption of a wide range of proven water-conserving techniques and technologies, especially water-conserving forms of agricultural irrigation.

At the more difficult international level, efforts need to:
- Promote dialogue on basin-wide cooperation in such fields as information-sharing, capacity building, and technology transfers, as well as on regional development programs.
- Focus on achievable goals without getting stuck on rights and allocation issues.

Desertification and Land Degradation

Current trends
- Desertification and drought are problems of a global dimension that affect more than 900 million people in 100 countries, some of them among the least developed in the world.
- 3.6 billion hectares, 25 percent of the Earth's land area, are being affected by land-degradation. Desertification is occurring to some extent on 30 percent of irrigated areas, 47 percent of rainfed agricultural lands, and 73 percent of rangelands.
- An estimated 1.5-2.5 million hectares of irrigated land, 3.5-4.0 million hectares of rainfed agricultural land, and about 35 million hectares of rangelands lose all or part of their productivity every year due to land-degradation processes.

Underlying causes
- Complex interactions among physical, biological, political, social, cultural, and economic factors cause desertification.
- Population growth and the need for food production in ecologically fragile arid and semi-arid lands, is putting too much pressure on the ecosystems.
- Many land-use projects are designed with little understanding of the socioeconomic conditions of the population and the dynamics and sustainability of the natural-resource base.
- Inappropriate economic policies that undervalue natural resources and encourage misuse.

Projected impact of human activities on desertification
- By 2025 the number of people adversely affected by desertification is expected to double to 1.8 billion people.

Social and economic consequences of desertification
- Intensive population pressures and improper resource use degrade the land, reduce its productivity, decrease food security and health prospects, increase poverty, and increase pressures for large-scale migration. The annual income lost worldwide due to desertification is estimated to be $42 billion.
- Desertification and land degradation affect the regional and global energy balance, reduce carbon sequestration and storage, and increase carbon emission.
- Land degradation in dryland systems can lead to the loss of genetic and species diversity. Drylands contain a significant endowment of plant and animal species biodiversity, a vital source of genetic materials that include important sources of medical, commercial, and industrial products.
- Land degradation causes loss of productivity and impairment of aquatic ecosystems through sediment pollution, salt intrusion and general environmental degradation.

Technologies, policies, and measures to mitigate desertification
- Providing family planning, health, and education services (especially for women).
- Developing programs to eradicate poverty and promote alternative livelihood systems.
- Developing effective and sustainable uses of land and natural resources that do not endanger their future productivity.
- Integrating anti-desertification schemes into national environment and development planning.
- Involving beneficiaries in the planning and management of resources, to ensure equitable access.

Status of international agreement
- The Desertification Convention was originally signed by 116 countries in Paris in June 1994. The Convention came into force December 26, 1996, and 128 countries had ratified the convention by mid-1998. The first Conference of Parties (COP) was held in fall 1997 in Rome, Italy.

Deforestation and the Unsustainable Use of Forests

Current trends
- More than one-fifth of the world's tropical forests have been cleared since 1960. Tropical deforestation increased from 11.8 million hectares per year in the 1970s to 15.4 million hectares (0.8 percent of total natural forest cover) in the 1980s. Current rates of tropical deforestation are typically averaging about 0.7 percent per year.
- Continuing loss of old-growth habitat in many temperate and boreal forest ecosystems, with remaining semi-natural forest covering less than 0.8 percent of the original forest in Western Europe and 1-2 percent in the United States.
- Serious loss of forest quality in many temperate and boreal forests due to pollution and other injurious agents; the associated productivity losses in Eastern Europe alone are estimated at US$30 billion per year.
- Forest clearing and burning currently account for between 7 and 30 percent of annual atmospheric carbon emissions.

Underlying causes of change
- Population growth and increasing per capita demands for forest products are increasing pressures for forest exploitation and the conversion of forest lands to agriculture and other forms of development, such as mining and fossil fuel extraction.
- Market failures that undervalue both the benefits of forest ecosystems and the true costs of damages associated with forest exploitation and conversion.
- Policy failures that provide perverse incentives for forest degradation and destruction.
- Institutional failures that lead to insecure resource access rights for forest-dependent communities, and a lack of transparency in forest resource pricing and allocation processes which, in turn, encourages corruption and the misuse of forest resources.

Projected impact of human activities on forests
- Decreased global forest cover.
- Loss of soil fertility and increase in soil erosion from deforested areas.
- Loss of significant carbon storage.

Social and economic consequences of projected changes
- Loss of substantial biodiversity, with forests currently accounting for more than 80 percent of terrestrial biodiversity.
- Loss of environmental protection services for fragile sites and critical watersheds.
- Potential changes in local, regional, and global climatic patterns.
- Loss of resource access and sustainable income support for forest-dependent communities.
- Rent capture by a small elite reduces the scope for equitable social development.

Technologies, policies, and measures to reduce the loss of forests
- Integrated land-use planning to secure a more stable forest area, with conservation, protection, and natural and planted production forests.
- Community involvement in all aspects of forest management and planning.
- Developing markets for a wider range of forest goods and services, including carbon storage and watershed protection services.
- Low-impact harvesting technologies, less waste of harvested products, and experimentation with alternative fiber sources.
- Independent, third-party certification of the sustainability of forest management systems, to encourage sales of these products.

Status of international agreements
- The International Tropical Timber Agreement (ITTA) of 1983, renegotiated in 1994.
- The Convention on Biological Diversity, the Framework Convention on Climate Change, and the Convention to Combat Desertification.

Marine Environment and Resource Degradation

Current trends
- Coastal waters have been contaminated by land-based sources, particularly municipal wastes that cause eutrophication.
- Red tides have increased in distribution and frequency in many coastal seas, and there are links to eutrophication.
- Oceanic waters already show human impacts, both in terms of trace contaminants and measurable temperature and sea-level increase.
- Total marine fish production is leveling off as the landings of demersal fish have remained constant since the 1970s.
- More than two-thirds of the world's marine fish stocks are being fished at or beyond their level of maximum productivity.
- The Atlantic Ocean was fully fished in 1980, the Pacific Ocean will be by 1999, and the remaining large areas are still developing.
- Many fishery resources classified as overexploited in 1992 have been showing decreased yields for the last 20 years, and are now producing 6 million tons less than they did in 1985.

Underlying causes of change
- Overfishing.
- Inadequate waste management on land, particularly in rapidly growing coastal settlements.
- Destruction of natural cover of watersheds.

Projected impact of human activities on the oceans
- Increased extent of coastal areas becoming unsuitable for recreation and food production.
- Loss of coral reefs and mangroves.
- Contribution to sea-level rises.
- Collapse of additional fish stocks.

Social and economic consequences of projected changes
- Greater incidence of illness due to consumption of contaminated fish and shellfish.
- Decline in marine fisheries production, and increased prices resulting in lower per capita consumption, especially among the poor.
- Unemployment and social dislocation caused by the collapse of traditional fisheries.
- Decline in coastal tourism.
- Increased cost of coastal protection measures.

Technologies, policies, and measures to mitigate projected changes
- Improved management of fisheries, both capture and culture.
- Better waste management (implementation of the Washington Declaration).
- Improved monitoring of coastal waters to prevent health-related problems.

Status of international agreements
- U.N. Convention on Law of the Sea, first signed in 1982, came into force in 1994.
- Agreement for the Implementation of the Provision of the U.N. Convention on Law of the Sea Relating to the Conservation and Management of Straddling Fish Stocks and Highly Migratory Fish Stocks - New York, August 1995.

Persistent Organic Pollutants (POPS)

Current trends

- Persistent organic pollutants (POPs) are chemical substances that resist natural breakdown processes and bioaccumulate in fatty tissues at different levels of the food chain. POPs also are semi-volatile, enabling them to move long distances in the atmosphere.
- The ability of POPs to persist in the environment and travel long distances has resulted in the presence of POPs all over the world, even in regions where they have never been used.
- Most of the twelve POPs currently addressed in international negotiations have been banned or subjected to severe use restrictions in many countries for more than 20 years. Many of them, however, are still in use in many countries, and stockpiles of obsolete POPs exist in many parts of the world.

Underlying causes of issue

- POPs comprise a large number of chemicals that have a wide range of uses. The twelve targeted POPs are used primarily in industry, agriculture, and disease vector control. Nine of them are pesticides used for crops and/or public health vector control (e.g., control of malaria-carrying mosquitoes).
- POPs can be produced cheaply compared to most other industrial chemicals.

Social and economic consequences of use of POPs

- Humans can be exposed to POPs through diet, occupational accidents, and the environment. Exposure to very low doses of certain POPs can lead to cancer, damage to the central and peripheral nervous systems, diseases of the immune system, reproductive disorders, and interference with infant and child development.
- Human health impacts may be felt most acutely in populations that consume large amounts of fish (e.g., subsistence fishermen), since fish have a high fat content and thus can contain high concentrations of POPs.
- The accumulation of obsolete stockpiles of pesticides and toxic chemicals (particularly common in developing countries) can cause leaching of these chemicals into the soil, contaminating water resources used by both wildlife and people.

Technologies, policies, and measures for shifting to safer alternatives

- There is sufficient evidence of harm to wildlife and humans to demonstrate that international action is required to reduce the risk of POPs to health and environment.
- Shifting from POPs to chemical and non-chemical alternatives is the key to reducing the impact of these hazardous substances. A high priority is finding alternatives to hazardous chemicals for insect control.
- There are many safer chemical and non-chemical alternatives, but their development and dissemination will require time, money, and training. For example, replacing DDT (widely used to control malarial mosquitoes) with less-hazardous forms of insect control requires time to plan effective actions (e.g., integrated pest management systems, consisting of the sparing use of pest-specific pesticides and biological control methods).
- Many countries face barriers to identifying and controlling releases of POPs. These include high prices of some alternatives, the need for education and training on the hazardous nature of POPs, a lack of information on what alternatives are available, a lack of reliable data about the current uses of POPs in each country, and the need for regulations/infrastructure to manage the use of pesticides. In many cases, technology transfer and development assistance are needed to bring replacements into widespread use.

Status of international agreements

- Because of the global risks posed by the long-range transport of POPs, the international community is calling for global action to reduce and eliminate releases of these chemicals.
- The United Nations Environment Programme (UNEP) is leading the development of a global legally-binding agreement to minimize releases of POPs into the environment. The first meeting on such an agreement was held in Montreal in June 1998. The second round of talks is tentatively scheduled for early 1999, and the negotiations are expected to conclude by the year 2000.
- Twelve specific POPs are internationally recognized as requiring elimination and reduction: aldrin, chlordane, DDT, dieldrin, dioxins, endrin, furans, heptachlor, hexachlorobenzene, mirex, PCBs, and toxaphene. Scientific criteria will be developed for identifying other POPs that may be added to the list later.
- UNEP also has initiated actions on sharing information, evaluating and monitoring implemented strategies, alternatives to POPs, identification and inventories of PCBs, available destruction capacity, and other issues. UNEP and the Intergovernmental Forum on Chemical Safety (IFCS) also are convening awareness-raising workshops in developing countries and countries with economies in transition.

APPENDIX 3

International Scientific Assessments of Major Global Environmental Issues

Global Environmental Issue	Assessment
Climate Change	*1.* *Climate Change 1990:* *First Assessment Report of the Intergovernmental Panel on Climate Change (IPCC)* • The IPCC Scientific Assessment (Working Group I) • The IPCC Impacts Assessment (Working Group II) • The IPCC Response Strategies (Working Group III) *2.* *Climate Change 1992:* • The Supplementary Report to the IPCC Scientific Assessment (WG I) • The Supplementary Report to the IPCC Impacts Assessment (WG II) *3.* *Climate Change 1995:* *Second Assessment Report of the Intergovernmental Panel on Climate Change (IPCC)* • The Science of Climate Change (WG I) • Impacts, Adaptations and Mitigation of Climate Change: Scientific-Technical Analyses (WG II) • Economic and Social Dimensions of Climate Change (WG III) • The IPCC Second Assessment Synthesis of Scientific-Technical Information Relevant to Interpreting Article 2 of the UNFCCC 1995 *4.* *Technical Papers and Special Reports:* • Technologies, Policies and Measures for Mitigating Climate Change 1996 (WG II): Technical Paper I • An Introduction to Simple Climate Models used in the IPCC Second Assessment Report 1997 (WG I): Technical Paper II • Stabilization of Atmospheric Greenhouse Gases: Physical, Biological, and Socio-economic Implications 1997 (WG I): Technical Paper III • Implications of Proposed CO_2 Emission Limitations 1997 (WG I): Technical Paper IV • The Regional Impacts of Climate Change: An Assessment of Vulnerability 1998 (WG II): Special Report
Stratospheric Ozone Depletion	1. The Stratosphere 1981: Theory and Measurements, 1982. 2. Atmospheric Ozone 1985: Assessment of Our Understanding of the Processes Controlling its Present Distribution and Change, 1986. 3. Report of the International Ozone Trends Panel, 1988, 1990. 4. UNEP/WMO Scientific Assessment of Ozone Depletion, 1989, 1990. 5. UNEP/WMO Scientific Assessment of Ozone Depletion, 1991, 1992. 6. Methyl Bromide: Its Atmospheric Science, Technology, and Economics, 1992. 7. UNEP/WMO Scientific Assessment of Ozone Depletion, 1994, 1995. 8. UNEP/WMO Scientific Assessment of Ozone Depletion, 1998.
Desertification	UNEP, WMO: Interactions of Desertification and Climate, 1996.
Freshwater Degradation	UN/SEI: Comprehensive Freshwater Assessment, 1997.
Deforestation and Forest Degradation	FAO: Forests Resources Assessment, 1990.
Marine Environment and Resource Degradation	FAO: State of World Fisheries and Aquaculture, 1996.
Persistent Organic Pollutants	Ongoing POPs Assessment.
Biodiversity Loss	UNEP: Global Biodiversity Assessment, 1995.

APPENDIX 4

International Conventions on Global Environmental Issues

Convention	Objectives
UN Framework Convention on Climate Change (1992)	Article 2: Stabilize greenhouse gas concentrations in the atmosphere at a level that would prevent dangerous anthropogenic interference with the climate system. . .within a time-frame sufficient to allow ecosystems to adapt naturally to climate change, to ensure that food production is not threatened, and to enable economic development to proceed in a sustainable manner.
Kyoto Protocol (1997)	Industrialized countries have agreed to reduce their emissions of greenhouse gases by, on average, 5.2 percent during the commitment period 2008-2012, relative to 1990.
UN Convention on Biological Diversity (1992)	Conserve biological diversity, the sustainable use of its components, and the fair and equitable sharing of the benefits arising out of the utilization of genetic resources, including by appropriate access to genetic resources and by appropriate transfer of relevant technologies, taking into account all rights over those resources and technologies, and by appropriate funding.
Vienna Convention for the Protection of the Ozone Layer (1985)	Protect human health and the environment against adverse effects resulting or likely to result from human activities which modify or are likely to modify the ozone layer.
Montreal Protocol (1987) as adjusted and amended in London (1990), Copenhagen (1992), and Vienna (1995)	Protect the ozone layer by taking precautionary measures to control equitably total global emissions of substances that deplete it, *with the ultimate objective of their elimination* on the basis of developments in scientific knowledge, taking into account technical and economic considerations and bearing in mind the developmental needs of developing countries.
UN Convention to Combat Desertification (1994)	Combat desertification and mitigate the effects of drought in countries experiencing serious drought and/or desertification, particularly in Africa, through effective action at all levels, supported by international cooperation and partnership arrangements, in the framework of an integrated approach that is consistent with Agenda 21, with a view to contributing to the achievement of sustainable development in affected areas.
UN Convention on the Law of the Sea (1982)	Establish a legal order for the seas and oceans that will facilitate international communication, and promote the peaceful uses of the seas and oceans, the equitable and efficient utilization of their resources, the conservation of their living resources, and the study, protection and preservation of the marine environment.
UN Agreement on Straddling Fish Stocks and Highly Migratory Fish Stocks (1995)	Supplements the 1982 Law of the Sea Convention by reinforcing the management and enforcement powers of high seas fisheries management bodies and of their members. It introduces precautionary management methodology and requires that ecological and biodiversity concerns be addressed in management of these stocks.
Global Program of Action for the Protection of the Marine Environment from Land-Based Activities (1995)	Developed under UNEP's auspices, this program sets forth the approach by which nations can cooperate and build institutional capacity to achieve the aims of specific international marine agreements, such as the Law of the Sea, regional seas agreements, MARPOL, the Basel Convention, and the London Convention. It offers guidance for nations to establish targets to address a host of marine pollution issues.
UN Convention on the Law of the Non-Navigational Uses of International Watercourses (1997)	Provides a legal framework to ensure the utilization, conservation, management and protection of international watercourses and the promotion of optimal and sustainable utilization for present and future generations.
Convention on the Prior Informed Consent (PIC) Procedure for Certain Hazardous Chemicals and Pesticides in International Trade (1998)	Developed to provide notice and consent procedures surrounding the international trade in chemicals and pesticides by facilitating information about their characteristics, and by providing for a national decisionmaking process on their import and export.

APPENDIX 5

International Agreements on Global Forest Issues

Statement	Objective
Proposals for Action Agreed by the Intergovernmental Panel on Forests of the Commission on Sustainable Development, adopted by UNGASS Decision on Forests (1997)	In order to implement the Statement on Forest Principles, establishes 12 programs: 1. National forest and land-use plans 2. Underlying causes of deforestation 3. Traditional forest-related knowledge 4. Ecosystems affected by desertification and pollution 5. Needs of countries with low forest cover 6. Financial assistance and technology transfer 7. Forest assessment 8. Valuation of forest benefits 9. Criteria and indicators 10. Trade and the environment 11. International organizations 12. Legal mechanisms
Non-legally Binding Authoritative Statement of Principles for a Global Consensus on the Management, Conservation, and Sustainable Development of All Types of Forests (1992)	Contribute to the management, conservation, and sustainable development of forests and provide for their multiple and complementary functions and uses.

APPENDIX 6

Selected Readings

Global Environmental Assessments

Climate Change	1. *Climate Change 1995: Second Assessment Report of the Intergovernmental Panel on Climate Change* (IPCC). • *The Science of Climate Change* (WG I) - Cambridge University Press, Cambridge, UK, 1996. • *Impacts, Adaptations and Mitigation of Climate Change: Scientific-Technical Analyses* (WG II) - Cambridge University Press, New York, USA, 1996. • *Economic and Social Dimensions of Climate Change* (WG III) - Cambridge University Press, New York, USA, 1996. • *The IPCC Second Assessment Synthesis of Scientific-Technical Information Relevant to Interpreting Article 2 of the UNFCCC –* WMO, Geneva, 1996. 2. Technical Papers and Special Reports: • *Technologies, Policies, and Measures for Mitigating Climate Change 1996* (WG II): Technical Paper I, IPCC - WMO, Geneva, 1996. • *The Regional Impacts of Climate Change: An Assessment of Vulnerability 1998* (WG II): Special Report. Cambridge University Press, New York, USA, 1998.
Stratospheric Ozone Depletion	1. *Scientific Assessment of Ozone Depletion: 1994,* WMO Global Ozone Research and Monitoring Project Report No. 37 (NOAA, NASA, UNEP, WMO), WMO, 1995. 2. *Scientific Assessment of Ozone Depletion: 1998,* WMO Global Ozone Research and Monitoring Project Report No. 44 (UNEP, WMO, NOAA, NASA, European Union) WMO, 1999.
Desertification	*UNEP: World Atlas of Desertification,* UNEP, Nairobi, and Edward Arnold, London, 1992.
Freshwater Degradation	*Comprehensive Assessment of the Freshwater Resources of the World,* UN/SEI, WMO, Geneva, 1997.
Deforestation and Forest Degradation	*Forest Resources Assessment,* FAO, Rome, 1990.
Marine Environment and Resource Degradation	*The State of World Fisheries and Aquaculture 1996,* FAO, Rome, 1997.
Persistent Organic Pollutants	Ongoing POPs assessment (initiated by UNEP Governing Council in May 1995).
Biodiversity Loss	*Global Biodiversity Assessment,* UNEP, Cambridge University Press, Cambridge, UK, 1995.

United Nations

	1. *AGENDA 21.* Adopted by the UN Conference on Environment and Development (UNCED) at Rio de Janeiro, 13 August, 1992. 2. *Global Environment Outlook* (GEO). UNEP, Oxford University Press, New York, 1997.

The World Bank

	1. *Expanding the Measure of Wealth: Indicators of Environmentally Sustainable Development,* The World Bank, Washington, D.C., 1997. 2. *Five Years after Rio: Innovations in Environmental Policy,* The World Bank, Washington, D.C., 1997.